Positive Affect Treatment for Depression and Anxiety

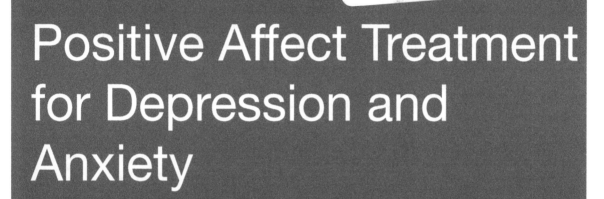

Positive Affect Treatment for Depression and Anxiety

WORKBOOK

ALICIA E. MEURET
HALINA J. DOUR
AMANDA G. LOERINC GUINYARD
MICHELLE G. CRASKE

OXFORD
UNIVERSITY PRESS

OXFORD
UNIVERSITY PRESS

Oxford University Press is a department of the University of Oxford. It furthers the University's objective of excellence in research, scholarship, and education by publishing worldwide. Oxford is a registered trade mark of Oxford University Press in the UK and certain other countries.

Published in the United States of America by Oxford University Press
198 Madison Avenue, New York, NY 10016, United States of America.

Library of Congress Cataloging-in-Publication Data
Names: Meuret, Alicia E., editor.
Title: Positive affect treatment for depression and anxiety : workbook /
Alicia E. Meuret, Halina J. Dour, Amanda G. Loerinc Guinyard, Michelle G. Craske.
Description: New York, NY, United States of America : Oxford University Press, [2022] |
Series: Treatments that work | Includes bibliographical references and index.
Identifiers: LCCN 2022003279 (print) | LCCN 2022003280 (ebook) |
ISBN 9780197548608 (paperback) | ISBN 9780197548615 (epub) |
ISBN 9780197548639
Subjects: LCSH: Depression, Mental—Treatment. |
Anxiety disorders—Treatment. | Positive reframing (Psychotherapy)
Classification: LCC RC537 .P659 2022 (print) | LCC RC537 (ebook) |
DDC 616.85/27—dc23/eng/20220314
LC record available at https://lccn.loc.gov/2022003279
LC ebook record available at https://lccn.loc.gov/2022003280

DOI: 10.1093/med-psych/9780197548608.001.0001

9 8 7 6 5 4 3 2 1

Clip arts used are from shutterstock.com

Printed by Marquis, Canada

One of the most difficult problems confronting patients with various disorders and diseases is finding the best help available. Everyone is aware of friends or family who have sought treatment from a seemingly reputable practitioner, only to find out later from another doctor that the original diagnosis was wrong or the treatments recommended were inappropriate or perhaps even harmful. Most patients, or family members, address this problem by reading everything they can about their symptoms, seeking out information on the Internet or aggressively "asking around" to tap knowledge from friends and acquaintances. Governments and health care policymakers are also aware that people in need do not always get the best treatments—something they refer to as *variability in health care practices*.

Now health care systems around the world are attempting to correct this variability by introducing *evidence-based practice*. This simply means that it is in everyone's interest that patients get the most up-to-date and effective care for a particular problem. Health care policymakers have also recognized that it is very useful to give consumers of health care as much information as possible, so that they can make intelligent decisions in a collaborative effort to improve physical health and mental health. This series, Treatments *That Work*, is designed to accomplish just that. Only the latest and most effective interventions for particular problems are described, in user-friendly language. To be included in this series, each treatment program must pass the highest standards of evidence available, as determined by a scientific advisory board. Thus, when individuals suffering from these problems, or their family members, seek out an expert clinician who is familiar with these interventions and decides that they are appropriate, patients will have confidence they are receiving the best care available. Of course, only your health care professional can decide on the right mix of treatments for you.

Anhedonia refers to loss of interest or joy in usual activities, and is commonly experienced in the context of depression and anxiety as well as other conditions. Positive Affect Treatment is a program specifically designed to increase interest or joy in usual activities for individuals with depression or anxiety. The program includes three main sets of exercises.

The first, Actions Toward Feeling Better, involves ways to increase engagement in activities even if one doesn't really feel like it combined with subsequent recounting of the experience in order to savor the positive moments. The second, Attending to the Positive, involves a set of cognitive exercises for finding the positives in everyday situations. The third, Building Positivity, involves intentions and actions toward appreciative joy, gratitude, kindness, and generosity. Each component builds on the others to increase interest and pleasure in usual activities. Explanations are provided in each chapter for why certain techniques or practices are employed. Positive Affect Treatment will be an indispensable resource for individuals with depression or anxiety who are struggling to find enjoyment in life.

David H. Barlow, Editor-in-Chief,
Treatments *That Work*
Boston, MA

Contents

Psychoeducation

Case Examples

Meet Joy . . .

 Joy is a 53-year-old lawyer who lives with her husband of 18 years and two teenage children. Over the past five years, she has found herself becoming more and more depressed, irritable, and exhausted. Joy used to love to entertain, but she no longer feels the desire to meet with friends. She has begun turning down plans and not returning phone calls. She sometimes even avoids interactions with her husband and children. Joy wishes that she had the desire to engage with friends and family, but the idea of organizing gatherings or even meeting a friend for coffee feels overwhelming to her. While her work has not suffered yet, Joy feels that she needs to put in an increasing amount of time and effort to complete the same tasks. She notices that she is delegating more and more work she previously enjoyed and took pride in, such as meeting new clients or organizing happy hours with colleagues. Her husband and children have commented on her retreating to the bedroom after work. Instead of finding joy in cooking

meals together, she prefers to order take-out. Joy's low energy became worse after she stopped her daily exercise, an activity she loved in the past. She frequently feels hopeless and fears that she may lose her job if her motivation and drive continue to be low. Joy often has thoughts such as "what's the point of trying?" and "nothing will help." She spends more than three hours per day on her computer watching random TV shows to turn her mind off, but it only makes her mood worse. Additionally, she seeks reassurance from her husband that something must be physically wrong with her, which frustrates him and leads to arguments.

Joy underwent extensive medical testing for her fatigue, all of which were inconclusive. More recently, her primary care physician suggested that she seek treatment for depression. After some time, Joy agreed to consider therapy because she has become frustrated by her low mood and lack of energy. She also hopes that she can experience excitement and happiness again.

Meet Felix . . .

 Felix is a 26-year-old unemployed, non-binary individual, whose pronouns are he/him/his. He is seeking treatment due to feeling depressed. Felix has suffered from depression for as long as he can remember which has affected his functioning for years. As a result, Felix often missed high school and college classes due to a lack of energy and low mood. He also has a history of difficulty sleeping due to his inability to control racing thoughts about the past. All of this has led to dropping out of community college and difficulty maintaining jobs. After moving to a new town, Felix got a job working as a security guard. However, after two months, he began missing days of work due to his low mood and he was subsequently let go. Felix has struggled to look for jobs due to his low motivation and negative thoughts, such as "I won't enjoy any work I do." Felix has one close friend with whom he often talked over the phone but stopped because he felt he had nothing interesting to say. He occasionally has Zoom calls with his mother. He would like to make new friends but does not think that anyone would want to meet him or spend time with him. He has thoughts such as, "I'm too depressed for anyone to want to spend time with me, and I won't have fun anyways."

Additionally, Felix has repetitive thoughts that make him "stuck" and unable to engage in fun activities. Felix used to enjoy watching movies, gardening, and cooking; however, now he doesn't seem able to start an activity. Instead, he stays in his apartment, playing video games for hours. He increasingly finds it difficult to go to the grocery store or do other essential errands. Even taking a *walk around his neighborhood feels difficult for him. Felix continuously feels as though he won't enjoy any activity. He wants to feel excited about meeting new people again and find a job. However, his problems feel so vast that he does not know where to begin to solve them.*

Joy and Felix will be going on this journey through this treatment with you.

What Is Anhedonia, or Low Positivity?

People who are anxious, depressed, or stressed often experience a variety of negative emotions (e.g., anger, irritability, frustration, sadness, fear, or panic). They also might feel certain physical sensations, such as feeling on edge, difficulty with concentration, or feeling the urge to protect themselves, even in the absence of actual danger.

> **Anhedonia** = persistently low levels of positive emotions.

People who experience many negative emotions often have persistently low levels of positive emotions too, even in situations that are typically considered rewarding or positive. **Persistently low levels of positive emotions are referred to as anhedonia**. We will use this term throughout this workbook. For example, it can be hard for someone with anhedonia to look forward to positive events, feel good when there is a positive event, and know how to make themselves feel more positive. It is as if the mood system that regulates positive emotions is not working so well.

There are two mood systems that regulate emotions—positive and negative. The positive mood system is sometimes referred to as the reward or appetitive system.

1. The positive mood system is responsible for positive emotions, like excitement, joy, love, happiness, and satisfaction. It drives us to achieve goals and find rewards.
2. It is also the system guiding us when we socialize and laugh with friends, accept praise, or work hard to complete a task that is important to us. The positive system energizes us to put in the effort, to get motivated, to feel interested, and to imagine positive outcomes. It holds our interest, giving us a feeling of pride when the goal is achieved. That is why it is also called the appetitive system.

Anhedonia occurs when there is a deficit in this system.

There are three components of the positive mood system: (1) wanting, (2) liking, and (3) learning of positive experiences. The anticipation of or motivation to obtain positive outcomes—often referred to as the **wanting** component—drives our interest, imagination, and effort to engage in future positive experiences (like the expectation of having a good time with friends and putting in the effort to find the right venue for a get-together). Savoring of reward—often referred to as the **liking** component—drives our pleasure in the moment (like feeling good as we enjoy the time with our friends, and even afterward, when reflecting on the good time we had). It also helps us notice and appreciate the positive. **Learning** how to get positive outcomes is what helps us continue to feel positive emotions in the future (like learning that if we reach out to our friends, there is a good chance that they will respond positively to the invitation). The treatment described in this workbook addresses all three of these components—wanting, liking, and learning about positive experiences!

A second system—the negative mood system—is also core to our well-being. It drives us to avoid punishments and threats. So, when we face challenging situations, such as being criticized, being directly threatened, or hearing scary news, it is our negative mood system that becomes activated. It then prepares us to face the challenge by making us very alert and attentive to danger by fueling our bodies to respond to the danger, and it prepares us to fight, flee, or freeze (sometimes doing nothing is protective). That is why it is also called the defensive system. It produces negative emotions like fear, panic, distress, anxiety, anger, and sadness.

The positive and negative mood systems are essential for our survival. We need one system to protect ourselves from danger and the other to accomplish our goals and feel satisfied and happy. And we are continually balancing between these two systems depending on what is happening in our lives. Is it a time to protect ourselves and become defensive, or is it a time to reach out, explore, and find joy?

Although the positive and negative systems are linked, they are also independent, meaning that, someone can have positive emotions without having negative emotions—such as feeling joy after receiving an unexpected gift without feeling undeserving. It is also possible to have strong negative emotions without positive emotions, such as feeling sadness over the loss of a loved one. And one can have positive and negative emotions at the same time—such as the thrill and excitement of receiving an award at a public event combined with fear and anxiety about giving the acceptance speech for the award, or the joyful anticipation of taking a bubble bath mixed with feelings of guilt.

What Are the Consequences of Anhedonia?

At times, we all have trouble feeling positive emotions like happiness, mastery, interest, or pride. However, research shows that persistently low levels of positive mood are harmful to our well-being. The lack of drive from the positive mood system makes it challenging to maintain productivity and social relationships. The lack of in-the-moment enjoyment of previously rewarding or positive activities further reduces drive and motivation. People with anhedonia can experience a loss of purpose and a sense of hopelessness. They sometimes can even have an increased desire to end their life.

As previously mentioned, individuals with anhedonia can experience difficulties with any or all three components of the positive mood system: wanting, liking, and learning of positive experiences.

Difficulties with Wanting

Growing scientific evidence shows that anhedonia is associated with **less interest** in, **less motivation** in, and **less effort** to obtain positive outcomes or rewards. Examples include showing reduced interest and effort toward food, physical comfort, social praise, emotional connections, and valued accomplishments in life. In day-to-day life, this could mean having a really hard time preparing a meal for dinner, getting oneself ready and presentable for a social gathering, or working toward a promotion at work. The consequence is that the person with anhedonia misses out on many opportunities for rewards, which are essential to our mood and well-being. We need to feel rewarded to motivate us to do the important things in our lives, and without those feelings, there is little drive to continue. Having less motivation is directly linked to having **more difficulty imagining positive future events**. If we don't know what leads to positive emotions or outcomes, it's hard to imagine them happening.

Difficulties with Liking

Anhedonia influences our attention and limits what we notice. For example, someone with anhedonia might have a **hard time noticing**

anything positive in their day-to-day life. This includes stressful events. Of course, stressful events usually make all of us feel more negative, anxious, or worried (that's our negative defensive system coming into play), but recovery from stressors is greatly helped by finding the positive. An example is noticing the fresh smell of the air and the earth when it is raining. We recover more quickly from stress when we can find the positive even in some of the most challenging conditions. Yet, anhedonia makes it very hard to notice the positive, appreciate the positive, and feel positive emotions, therefore making it hard to recover from stressors. Someone with anhedonia may only focus on the negative in a positive (or neutral) situation. For example, a person with anhedonia may notice running out of cookies at a food drive as a sign of failure rather than success. If we continuously fail to identify the positive in positive, neutral, or negative situations, our motivation to stay engaged will be compromised. Thus, even when people with anhedonia notice the positive, they may struggle to appreciate it and feel positive emotions in response to it. For example, they may no longer find going to ball games with their kids fun, or fishing as something relaxing to do, or making crafts enjoyable. **Difficulties appreciating the positive and feeling positive emotions** are also symptoms of anhedonia.

Difficulties with Learning

Anhedonia is also associated with **trouble learning what is likely to lead to positive outcomes** due to the lowered drive to experience reward in the first place. For example, the person with anhedonia may not know what to say or do in a social situation in order to feel connected and supported by others. Or someone with anhedonia may struggle to realize that smiling at colleagues can contribute to better relationships at work and a possible promotion.

Putting it all together, anhedonia (or persistently low positive emotions) is associated with difficulties imagining and working on getting positive outcomes or rewards (wanting), difficulties noticing and appreciating the positive when it does occur (liking), and difficulties learning the connection between the aforementioned (learning). In the case of Joy, introduced earlier in this chapter, she may have loved exercising in the past but stopped because she could not imagine it feeling pleasurable, or it was not enjoyable when she tried. As a result, she decided that there would be no worth in trying again.

Anhedonia leads to lowered activation in the part of our nervous system that we need to feel positive emotions. It also leads to less activation in the parts of our brain that understand the importance of rewards, leading to **low positive mood**. In addition to the difficulties described earlier, research suggests that anhedonia can impair executive functioning such as planning, decision-making, memory, and concentration. This means that a person with anhedonia may not only lack the motivation to do something rewarding but also find it difficult to remember, plan, or focus on the steps that would be needed.

Anhedonia affects reward **wanting** (motivation, effort, imagining, interest), **liking** (noticing, appreciating, feeling positive emotions), and **learning** (understanding how to obtain positive outcomes).

 For example, Joy may not only feel unmotivated to go to the store to buy food to make dinner for her family but also has difficulties deciding which store to go to or what to buy. Or when she is at the store, she may have difficulties following through with her plan because she feels no excitement.

Figure 1.1 summarizes the core terms presented in this chapter. We include symbols that represent the core deficits in wanting, liking, and learning. The symbols will be used throughout the workbook so you know what reward deficit is being targeted.

To illustrate the symbols in Figure 1.1, we use the example of "Having dinner with a friend." The person who "wants" to go out with a friend imagines that eating dinner with a friend leads to the reward of an enjoyable evening. They will "like" the dinner and enjoy the food and company. They will notice emotions of joy, connectedness, and appreciation. They will "learn" to form associations between imagining going out with a friend, taking the steps to plan a dinner out with a friend, meeting the friend, and feeling positive emotions. Learning these associations will lead to additional get-togethers in the future.

Individuals with anhedonia do not necessarily experience deficits in all three components. They may only experience difficulties in the wanting area. For example, Joy may imagine a phone call with a friend to be too burdensome to do, but she enjoys it after getting on the phone. If this is the case, she would want to focus on techniques targeting wanting first.

Deficits In	Reward System	
• Getting motivated to do positive activities • Putting effort into positive activities • Imagining positive outcomes • Being interested in the positive	• Reward motivation • Reward anticipation	 **Wanting**
• Noticing the positive • Appreciating the positive • Feeling positive emotions	• Reward attainment	 **Liking**
• Learning what leads to rewards • Learning how to obtain rewards	• Reward learning	 **Learning**

Figure 1.1

Parts of the reward system and associated deficits of anhedonia.

Clipart sourced from Microsoft PowerPoint.

To find where each component is targeted in this treatment, search for the symbols. Chapter 2 provides an overview of the skills taught in this program and the targeted reward component.

What Does Science Say About Treating Anhedonia?

Until now, standard psychological and pharmacological treatments for anxiety and depression have had limited effects on anhedonia. They successfully reduce negative emotions, but most individuals with anhedonia continue to report a lack of interest or joy in positive activities at the end of treatment. This state of affairs may have arisen because most existing psychological treatments focus on reducing negative emotions without focusing on improving positive emotions. This is partly due to lack of a guiding science for improving positivity.

The latest advances in behavioral and biological science have shed light on the specific processes involved in anhedonia. We developed a new psychological treatment called the **Positive Affect Treatment** or **PAT** (presented in this workbook) that specifically targets problems with wanting, liking, and reward learning (*affect* is another term for emotion or feelings).

Like many evidence-based treatments for emotional disorders, the current treatment takes a cognitive–behavioral approach. In this approach, people work on their behaviors and thoughts (i.e., cognitions) to change how they feel. This approach was built on science and theory that *what you do* and *how you think* directly affects *how you feel*. Science has shown that cognitive–behavioral therapies effectively treat a multitude of mental health disorders and conditions, including anxiety disorders, depressive disorders, eating disorders, psychosis, chronic pain, substance use, and sleep. Now, anhedonia can be added to this list!

The skills included in this workbook are evidence-based, meaning they have been tested in randomized controlled trials and shown to improve positive emotions in individuals who are anxious, stressed, or depressed and also experience anhedonia. In our most recent investigation, we found that the therapy skills included in this workbook were more successful in increasing positive emotions than an alternative cognitive–behavioral therapy that focused on reducing negative emotions. Specifically, the majority of the participants who received PAT ended up in the normal range of positive emotions, using a validated scale of positivity. Notably, PAT was more successful than the alternative treatment in decreasing symptoms of depression, anxiety, and stress. It also reduced suicidality more than traditional cognitive–behavioral therapy.[1]

What Are Common Psychiatric Conditions Associated with Anhedonia?

Anhedonia is commonly present in the majority of psychiatric conditions. For example, in our studies, most individuals who suffered from anhedonia also met the diagnostic criteria for an anxiety or depressive disorder. Examples include anxiety disorders such as generalized anxiety disorder (GAD), social anxiety disorder, panic disorder, obsessive–compulsive disorder (OCD), and posttraumatic stress disorder (PTSD). Major depressive disorder is another disorder characterized by low positive affect.

---

[1] Craske, M. G., Meuret, A. E., Ritz, T., Rosenfield, D., Treanor, M., & Dour, H. (2019). Positive Affect Treatment for Depression and Anxiety: A randomized clinical trial for a core feature of anhedonia. *Journal of Consulting and Clinical Psychology, 87,* 457–471.

Generalized Anxiety Disorder

Individuals with GAD worry about a variety of different topics (e.g., their own health, the health of family members, finances, being on time, success in the future). Usually, this worry is disproportionate to reality, is future-oriented, and is present even if things are going well. Individuals with GAD tend to worry for the majority of most days and find it difficult to stop and control their worries. To try to reduce the worries, individuals with GAD engage in behaviors such as frequent checking on loved ones, procrastination, and excessive internet searching.

Social Anxiety Disorder

Individuals with social anxiety disorder experience anxiety in situations involving other people, where they may be observed, judged, or evaluated. To reduce or avoid this anxiety, they may stay away from social gatherings or events, such as parties, meetings, job interviews, public speaking engagements, and dates. While this avoidance reduces anxiety in the short term, it maintains social anxiety in the long term.

Panic Disorder

Individuals with panic disorder experience panic attacks. Panic attacks are sudden rushes of intense fear accompanied by physical sensations (e.g., sweating, racing heart, heart palpitations, dizziness, shortness of breath, lightheadedness, trembling or shaking, feeling of choking, chest pain, numbness, nausea, chills, hot flashes). Individuals with panic disorder find the physical sensations extremely distressing and therefore avoid all things that may result in a panic attack. People with panic disorder may avoid activities such as drinking caffeinated beverages, going to crowded places, using public transportation, exercising, and being in wide-open spaces.

Obsessive–Compulsive Disorder

Individuals with OCD often have intrusive thoughts (i.e., obsessions) that are distressing (e.g., violent images, believing that a certain number has meaning). To reduce the distress associated with the intrusive thoughts, they frequently engage in behaviors (i.e., compulsions) that are disruptive to daily functioning and can be time-consuming (e.g., repeatedly saying a phrase until the image goes away, only choosing the fifth item on a shelf).

Examples of compulsions are frequent hand washing, repeatedly checking locks, and excessive organizing.

Posttraumatic Stress Disorder

Some individuals who have experienced a traumatic event develop PTSD. Examples of traumatic events are assault, war, a severe car accident, and abuse. Symptoms of PTSD include distressing and intrusive memories of the traumatic event, nightmares, flashbacks, hypervigilance, and increased physiological arousal. Individuals with PTSD also may avoid people, places, and activities that remind them of the trauma and engage in safety behaviors, such as always sitting near an exit.

Depressive Disorders (Major Depressive Disorder, Persistent Depressive Disorder)

Individuals with depressive disorders often feel down or sad and have lost interest or pleasure in activities they once enjoyed. They often experience low energy, hopelessness, a change in appetite, either sleeping too much or too little, thoughts of worthlessness, and irritability. It is challenging for individuals with depression to engage in activities, resulting in social isolation, spending time in bed, and canceling plans.

Other Disorders

Substance use disorder, psychotic disorders (e.g., schizophrenia), and bipolar disorder are also commonly associated with anhedonia. People may also experience anhedonia without meeting the diagnostic criteria for a psychiatric disorder.

CHAPTER 2 ▸ How Will This Therapy Work for You?

Is This Treatment the Right Fit for You?

Many psychotherapies are available to choose from, so knowing which treatment is the right fit can be difficult. Each therapy has its own set of symptoms to target and skills to offer. In this treatment, we offer you a variety of skills to target your low mood. To help you determine whether this treatment is the right fit for you, it can be helpful to answer the questions on Exercise 2.1: Treatment Fit Assessment. You may photocopy this exercise from the book or download multiple copies at the Treatments *That Work™* website (www.oxfordclinicalpsych.com/PAT).

If you answered "yes" to most of these questions, this treatment can help you. PAT is uniquely designed to increase the frequency, variety, and intensity of positive emotions like pride, excitement, joy, curiosity, amusement, and contentment.

In addition to figuring out whether this treatment is right for you, it is also important to ask whether this treatment is right for you *right now*. The yes/no statements on Exercise 2.2: Treatment Timing Assessment can help to determine whether you are ready to start this treatment program. You may

	Reward System to Target				
	Yes	Wanting	Liking	Learning	Exercise to Practice
Are you having difficulty feeling positive emotions, like love, joy, curiosity, pride, and excitement?	☐		X		Labeling Emotions
Do you have difficulty noticing the positive in your day to day?	☐		X	X	Finding the Silver Linings
Do you tend to dismiss the positive?	☐		X	X	Gratitude
Do others tell you that you don't give yourself enough credit?	☐		X	X	Taking Ownership
Do you find yourself attributing good things to luck rather than your own doing?	☐		X	X	Taking Ownership
Are you more likely to imagine negative outcomes in the future than positive outcomes?	☐	X		X	Imagining the Positive
Have you stopped engaging in pleasant or enjoyable activities?	☐	X	X	X	Actions Toward Feeling Better
Are you finding it hard to find pleasure in activities you once enjoyed or think you should enjoy?	☐		X	X	Savoring / Generosity
Do you have a hard time getting motivated and excited about activities you once enjoyed or tasks that gave you a sense of accomplishment?	☐	X			Designing Positive Activities
Have you struggled to feel connected with others, including emotions of empathy, love, or compassion?	☐		X	X	Appreciative Joy / Loving-Kindness

Exercise 2.1

Treatment Fit Assessment

Clipart sourced from Microsoft PowerPoint.

	Yes	No
I can commit to completing practice assignments at home nearly every day (at least 3x/week).	☐	☐
I am not engaging in another treatment that will interfere with my ability to engage in this treatment.	☐	☐
I am not experiencing elevations in other symptoms that take priority over this treatment (e.g., suicidality, psychosis, mania, substance abuse).	☐	☐

Exercise 2.2

Treatment Timing Assessment

photocopy this exercise from the book or download multiple copies at the Treatments *That Work*™ website (www.oxfordclinicalpsych.com/PAT).

If you answered "yes" to each of these statements, then you are ready to start PAT! This workbook will walk you through the next steps of treatment. Please note, if you are experiencing elevations in other symptoms or conditions that take priority (e.g., suicidality, psychosis, mania, substance abuse), it is important that you seek treatment for those with a licensed health care provider. To find someone appropriate, we recommend that you set up an appointment with your primary care provider to ask about these symptoms and request a referral. **It is essential that if you have elevated thoughts of wanting to hurt yourself, seek immediate care by calling 911 or visiting the nearest emergency room.**

Structure of Treatment: What to Expect

PAT was developed to increase the number, frequency, and intensity of positive emotions. Therefore, all of the tools that you will be given in this therapy were designed and proven to do just that. Figure 2.1 provides an overview of the skills and targeted parts of the positive mood system in the respective modules and chapters of this workbook.

In the rest of this chapter, we briefly describe each module of the treatment and why we chose it to improve positive mood. You can find more in-depth information in the respective chapters of this workbook.

The What and the Why of the Treatment Modules

In this treatment, you will be introduced to the modules as presented in Figure 2.1. The treatment skill sets (covered in Chapters 5 through 7)

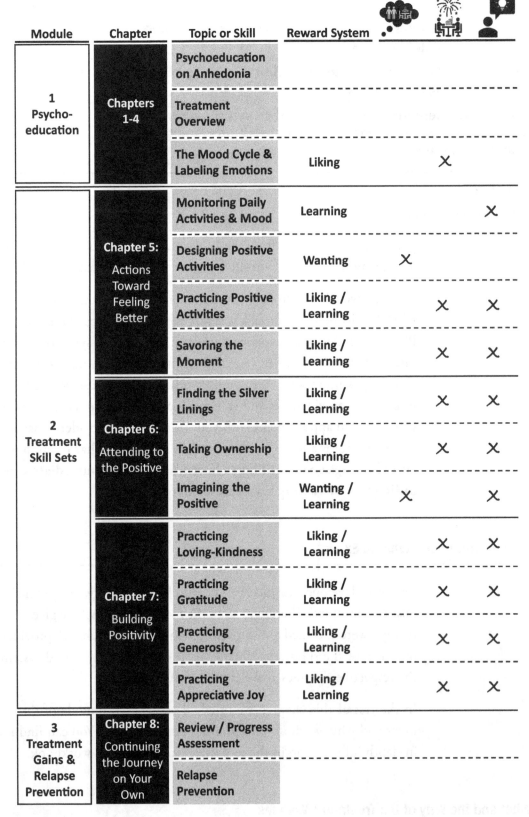

Module	Chapter	Topic or Skill	Reward System		
1 Psycho-education	Chapters 1-4	Psychoeducation on Anhedonia			
		Treatment Overview			
		The Mood Cycle & Labeling Emotions	Liking	X	
2 Treatment Skill Sets	Chapter 5: Actions Toward Feeling Better	Monitoring Daily Activities & Mood	Learning		X
		Designing Positive Activities	Wanting	X	
		Practicing Positive Activities	Liking / Learning	X	X
		Savoring the Moment	Liking / Learning	X	X
	Chapter 6: Attending to the Positive	Finding the Silver Linings	Liking / Learning	X	X
		Taking Ownership	Liking / Learning	X	X
		Imagining the Positive	Wanting / Learning	X	X
	Chapter 7: Building Positivity	Practicing Loving-Kindness	Liking / Learning	X	X
		Practicing Gratitude	Liking / Learning	X	X
		Practicing Generosity	Liking / Learning	X	X
		Practicing Appreciative Joy	Liking / Learning	X	X
3 Treatment Gains & Relapse Prevention	Chapter 8: Continuing the Journey on Your Own	Review / Progress Assessment			
		Relapse Prevention			

Figure 2.1

Overview of skills in the modules and chapters.

Clipart sourced from Microsoft PowerPoint.

target at least one part of the positive system to help you experience more positive mood.

Module 1: Psychoeducation

Chapter 1: Is It Difficult for You to Feel Positive Emotions?

Chapter 1 provides education on what anhedonia is. To recap, anhedonia is a term used to describe when someone is experiencing low positive mood. It describes someone who has difficulties: (1) being interested in previously enjoyable activities, (2) getting motivated or putting effort into doing positive activities, or (3) imagining future events more positively (wanting). Anhedonia is also used to describe when someone has difficulty noticing or appreciating the positive or finding it difficult feeling positive emotions (liking). Consequently, individuals with anhedonia tend to have fewer positive or pleasant activities built into their day because they struggle to learn what leads to rewards and how to obtain rewards (learning). It is for these reasons that certain individuals struggle to feel positive emotions. Therefore, each treatment skill set is designed to target at least one of these challenges.

Chapter 2: How Will This Therapy Work for You?

Chapter 2 explains how this therapy will work for you.

Chapter 3: Let's Get Started!

Chapter 3 discusses how you can get the most out of this treatment, such as how to use the exercise sheets, between-session assignments, suggested treatment schedule, and symptom tracking.

Chapter 4: The Triad of Feelings, Thoughts, and Actions

Chapter 4 provides additional education on what positive mood is, compared to negative mood. You will learn about the mood cycle and the importance of labeling emotions, which are foundational skills. The latter will help you strengthen your ability to verbally express what you notice and feel (liking). After some practice, you will dive into the three treatment skill sets of this therapy. Each will provide you with a set of behavioral and thinking skills to enhance your experience of positive emotions.

Module 2: Treatment Skill Sets

Chapter 5: Actions Toward Feeling Better

You will start with your behavior in this first treatment skill set. As you will soon learn, what you *do* has a direct impact on how you *feel*, and taking *actions toward feeling better* will be an effective and surefire way to improve your mood. This module will not only help you build positive activities in your life (wanting), it will also teach you how to get the most out of those activities (learning). You will begin to incorporate more positive activities into your week, and you will learn how to *savor* those positive activities (liking).

Science has demonstrated a clear link between engaging in these activities and improved mood. Our behavior skill set targets all three aspects of the positive system—liking, wanting, and learning. The goal is to build a life with more positive and meaningful activities and learn how to notice, appreciate, and savor them. You will also learn what is likely to lead to reward (learning).

Chapter 6: Attending to the Positive

The second skill set provides you with thinking skills, which will help you learn to pay attention to the positive. This skill set was specifically designed to target three common thinking traps that people with low positive mood experience:

1. Difficulty recognizing positive aspects of a situation (Skill: *Finding the Silver Linings*)
2. Not taking credit for doing something well (Skill: *Taking Ownership*)
3. Struggling with looking forward to or imagining positive events (Skill: *Imagining the Positive*)

With *Finding the Silver Linings*, you will identify positive aspects of various situations to train your mind to notice the positive. In *Taking Ownership*, you will recognize ways that you contribute to events going well in order to understand that what you do well is a blueprint for obtaining the positive in future events. These skills aim to help you recognize the positive that already exists in your day-to-day life and your contributions. This is important because we cannot appreciate what we have (liking) or know what steps to take in the future (learning) without acknowledging what is already present. In other words, knowing what you did to contribute to something going well can act as a blueprint for future activities. Many people struggle to envision future events going well for them. This is limiting their motivation and effort to engage in future positive activities. In *Imagining the Positive*, you will practice imagining future events in a more positive light. This will train your brain to start doing so more naturally.

All three skills will strengthen your ability to learn what leads to positive outcomes (learning). *Finding the Silver Linings* and *Taking Ownership* will particularly strengthen your ability to notice the positive (liking), while *Imagining the Positive* will be a particularly helpful skill to help you get motivated and energized (wanting)!

Chapter 7: Building Positivity

Our third treatment skill set includes four positive practices that science and Eastern philosophy have demonstrated to be effective in improving mood and enhancing positive affect. Those skills are *Loving-Kindness*, *Gratitude*, *Generosity*, and *Appreciative Joy*. These positive skills are a combination of behavioral and thinking skills that will enrich your life, especially your relationships.

In *Loving-Kindness*, you will offer loving and kind thoughts toward others, which enhances positive feelings of love, connection, and serenity. In *Appreciative Joy*, you will notice and appreciate the positive emotions that arise when you picture good things happening to others (e.g., loved ones, the world). *Gratitude* and *Generosity* are two additional skills that everyone is familiar with. Science has shown that engaging in both has strong benefits to one's own mood and well-being. All four skills target liking and learning of the positive, such as feeling positive emotions toward another person and learning how this feeling can be generated. They will help improve motivation and effort toward positive activities or acts of kindness. They will help you learn what leads to reward and how to obtain it.

Module 3: Treatment Gains and Relapse Prevention

The final module of this workbook (Chapter 8: Continuing the Journey After Treatment) is dedicated to ensuring that the gains you make during this treatment are maintained beyond treatment. This concluding chapter helps you troubleshoot general barriers that can occur along the way, such as lapses or lack of motivation. We want you to continue to enhance your emotional experience after treatment is over so that you are better equipped to achieve your life goals. To do that, it is important to recognize and anticipate that there will be inevitable barriers along the way. This final chapter will also help you assess your progress, distinguish between a lapse (an expected slip) and a relapse (a return to pretreatment levels), and identify when and how to seek additional help.

Chapter Structure

In every chapter, we start by providing you with an overview of skills, followed by why the skill set is important for this treatment and the science to support it. We understand that unless you fully understand the *what* and the *why* of those skills, the act of putting these skills into practice might not follow. Therapy requires practice, which takes time and energy that many of us only have so much of. Therefore, you must be fully aware of why devoting some of your limited time to practicing the skills in this treatment is so important.

Once we explain the science, we move on to introduce each skill within the set. We provide instructions and helpful exercise sheets to guide you through using them. Within every exercise sheet is a question that asks you to rate your mood before and after practicing the skills. Each skill will have a section on troubleshooting potential barriers and what homework to complete for the week. We recommend that you follow the suggested homework as closely as possible, including how often to practice. The old saying "Practice makes perfect" (or "Practice makes better") also applies to therapy.

Positive Affect Treatment (PAT) was designed to be flexible to meet the needs of individuals using it. Therefore, in the next chapter, we provide a recommended schedule with possible modifications to the treatment schedule.

Combining This Program with Other Treatments

There are several different methods of psychotherapy available. If you are engaging in another type of treatment to help reduce anxiety and depression symptoms, we recommend that you complete that treatment before starting this one. We also recommend that if you begin this program, you do not undergo similar treatment with a different therapist at the same time. It can become confusing if you are working with more than one therapist on the same problem. Therefore, we find it the most effective to do only one treatment program at a time. However, if you are doing a different kind of therapy (e.g., supportive psychotherapy, couples therapy, or family therapy), both treatments can likely be done at the same time. We encourage you to talk with your doctor or therapist about what makes the most sense regarding doing this treatment on its own or combining it with another treatment.

If you are taking medications for your symptoms of anxiety and depression, you may continue to take them during this program. Unless clinically necessary, we discourage increasing dosages of medication or beginning new medications during the course of treatment. This is because medication changes can interfere with therapeutic strategies and the evaluation of the therapy's effectiveness.

CHAPTER 3　Let's Get Started!

Getting the Most Out of This Treatment

We have designed this treatment with theory, science, and clinical experience in mind. This is true for the skills within this treatment and the order, layout, and structure of the treatment. For example, science and clinical experience strongly support that regular homework practice, especially with written and behavioral components, has a clear effect on treatment success. Therefore, we place a strong emphasis on everyday practice, and we have designed our exercise forms with this in mind. Similarly, the order of this treatment was designed with evidence from research in mind. Skills that rely on changing your behavior were chosen as the first set of skills to work on, given that science has shown that learning these skills early in treatment (and before learning about thinking skills) can have the most significant impact on treatment success, particularly for individuals with depression and anxiety. In other words, if you are feeling especially down or anxious and if you avoid or don't feel motivated to do things throughout the week, then starting with "Actions Toward Feeling

Better" (chapter 5) is likely most beneficial for you, as recommended in the schedule (treatment order) later in this chapter.

However, some individuals may notice that they already have a full week of activities that they enjoy. If this is you, it may be best to start with "Attending to the Positive" (chapter 6). Or suppose you have no difficulties with wanting (i.e., feeling motivated, interested, and imagining positive events). In that case, you can focus on skills promoting liking and learning.

Practicing skills at home is essential to make gains in therapy. Science has shown that clients who engage in regular homework during psychotherapy have better results than clients who do not complete homework. Therapy skills are no different than other skills you learn: They require frequent practice to see improvement. Ideally, you will be practicing your new skills daily. Therefore, this treatment's only cost is time and energy (and the price of this workbook). If you are working with a mental health professional, there may be some financial costs to receive care.

However, we acknowledge that not everyone has the time or energy to commit to this treatment, and that's okay. Therapy doesn't work overnight, and there are many reasons why someone might not be ready to start right now. Maybe you have a job or schedule that does not allow you to engage in regular homework practice, or maybe you are experiencing a family crisis that requires all of your time and energy right now. If time and energy are the reasons you cannot commit to therapy, it would be best to wait before starting this treatment.

Sometimes fear is the reason that someone doesn't believe they are ready for therapy. Fear of change or of the unknown is understandable. However, it is doubtful that this fear will go away if you continue to avoid it; instead, it will likely worsen. Other times, lack of motivation—which we know is common for people with low positive emotions—can be a reason someone does not engage in therapy. The Positive Affect Treatment (PAT) program (and your therapist, if you work with one) will help you manage your fear or lack of motivation by walking you through this therapy step by step and by teaching you new skills to improve how you feel.

No matter when you choose to start treatment, it is key that you try your best to follow through with it. This is true even if you start to feel better early in therapy. Similar to antibiotics, you'll want to get the full dose, regardless of how good you might be feeling early on. Doing so ensures that you have all of the skills you need to continue to improve and maintain your gains, even after the treatment is over and especially during inevitable future challenges.

Just remember that this therapy has been proven to improve mood, so whenever you are ready to start, PAT is here to guide you on the steps you need to start feeling more positive emotions again.

How to Use Exercise Forms

This book is filled with exercise forms to help you learn each skill. We encourage you to carefully read the instructions in each section to ensure that you can practice each skill as intended. Part of these assignments is to rate your positive mood before and after each exercise. Remember that this treatment was specifically built for individuals who struggle to notice or feel the positive. Tracking changes in your mood is an important component of PAT for several reasons. First, most people who struggle with low mood report that they have a hard time feeling positive emotions even when they do activities that are considered enjoyable (e.g., spending time with friends). However, training yourself to notice even small changes in your mood is an important step in being able to deepen your experience of positive emotions. As you track these small improvements in your mood, you are training yourself to notice the small changes in positive emotions, physical sensations, and thoughts that accompany positive mood shifts, and therefore, you are deepening your experience of positive emotions. Second, tracking your mood before and after various activities helps you learn which activities are associated with improvements in your mood. This strengthens learning on how to get positive results and improves your motivation to engage in these activities in the future. Therefore, before and after engaging in PAT activities, we will ask you to rate your mood on a scale from 0 (lowest mood) to 10 (highest mood).

When, for How Long, and How to Practice

Skills that we provide within each section are intended to be practiced daily (typically one exercise form per day) for the recommended time (e.g., one week). Even if a skill seems too simple or easy for you, we encourage you to practice it as suggested. Our recommendations are designed to give most people enough time to build mastery. Remember, the goal of homework is to transform these skills into habits.

However, the pace of the PAT program can be adapted to meet your needs. For example, if you need more time to practice, please take it, even after moving on to the next chapter—just make additional copies of the exercise forms. We do not, however, recommend that you spend more than an extra one to two weeks on each chapter before moving on to the next. Spending too long on a single chapter can affect your ability to learn all of the skills in the recommended time frame of 15 weeks. On the other hand, if you (and your therapist, if you are working with one) decide a more tailored approach is best for you (e.g., focusing on skills addressing deficits in motivation), your overall treatment time could be shorter.

It is best for you to practice some skills at the beginning or end of each day (e.g., *Finding the Silver Linings*, *Imagining the Positive*, *Gratitude*, *Loving-Kindness*, *Appreciative Joy*), while others will be best practiced during the day (e.g., *Practicing Positive Activities*, *Generosity*). Be mindful of not pushing your training to the end of the day when you do not feel motivated. You may end up not doing it at all. Research has shown that learning is most effective in the earlier parts of the day. When completing the exercise forms, it is best to do while practicing the skill to help the skills become habits. Place a few copies of your exercise forms in your car, office, or bag so you have them when you need them. Remember, you may photocopy exercise forms from the book or download multiple copies at the Treatments *That Work*™ website (www.oxfordclinicalpsych.com/PAT).

There is a tendency to practice a skill in one's mind versus actually writing down the responses. Practicing the skills by filling out the exercise forms in your workbook is important for learning early on. The art of writing has many benefits:

1. Writing can decrease the intensity of emotions, which helps when we are trying to work through thoughts and behaviors that directly affect our emotional experience.
2. Writing slows us down. Too often, we can find our minds racing or distractible, which can get in the way of building mastery.
3. Writing something down helps to consolidate memory (helps us to remember), which is essential for learning.

Suggested Treatment Schedule

PAT was designed to be both structured and flexible to meet your individual needs. Figure 3.1 illustrates a recommended schedule that we

Week	Chapter	Title
1	1-4	**Assessment** ▪ *Exercise 2.1: Treatment Fit Assessment* ▪ *Exercise 2.2: Treatment Timing Assessment* **Psychoeducation on Anhedonia and Treatment Overview** **The Mood Cycle** ▪ *Exercise 4.1: A Mood Cycle You Noticed* **Labeling Emotions** ▪ *Exercise 4.2: Positive Emotions Dial* **Actions Toward Feeling Better** ▪ *Exercise 5.1: Daily Activity and Mood Record*
2	5	**Actions Toward Feeling Better** ▪ *Exercise 5.1: Daily Activity and Mood Record* ▪ *Exercise 5.2: Positive Activity List* ▪ *Exercise 5.3: Positive Activity List through Mastery* ▪ *Exercise 5.4: My Positive Activity List*
3	5	**Actions Toward Feeling Better** ▪ *Exercise 5.5: Positive Activity Scheduling*
4-7	5	**Actions Toward Feeling Better** ▪ *Exercise 5.5: Positive Activity Scheduling* ▪ *Exercise 5.6: Savoring the Moment*
8	6	**Attending to the Positive** ▪ *Exercise 6.1: Finding the Silver Linings*
9	6	**Attending to the Positive** ▪ *Exercise 6.2: Taking Ownership*
10	6	**Attending to the Positive** ▪ *Exercise 6.3: Imagining the Positive*
11	7	**Building Positivity** ▪ *Exercise 7.1: Practicing Loving-Kindness*
12	7	**Building Positivity** ▪ *Exercise 7.2: Gratitude*
13	7	**Building Positivity** ▪ *Exercise 7.3: Generosity*
14	7	**Building Positivity** ▪ *Exercise 7.4: Appreciative Joy*
15	8	**Continuing the Journey on Your Own** ▪ *Exercise 8.1: My Progress Assessment* ▪ *Exercise 8.2: My Long-Term Goals* ▪ *Exercise 8.3: Maintaining My Gains* ▪ *Exercise 8.4: Overcoming Barriers*

Figure 3.1

Recommended treatment schedule.

encourage you to modify if you need more or less time on certain skills. If you work with a mental health professional, you can determine together whether to change the order to best meet your needs.

How Do You Know if You Improve?

It is important to begin to monitor your symptoms once you start treatment. That way, you will know whether you are improving, and this information can motivate you to keep going throughout treatment. Your therapist can help guide you to appropriate standardized questionnaires that assess positive mood, negative mood, and symptoms of anhedonia, depression, or anxiety.

CHAPTER 4

The Triad of Feelings, Thoughts, and Actions

What Is the Mood Cycle?

The mood cycle explains two things: It describes what leads to emotions and what emotions lead to. Let's start with what leads to emotions. How you think (thoughts), what you do (behaviors), and how your body feels (physical sensations) can directly change how you feel (emotions). The following examples will demonstrate how the triad of thoughts, behaviors, and physical sensations can directly influence our mood.

> **Mood cycle** = thoughts (thinking), behaviors (acting), and physical sensations (feeling).

Thoughts

Imagine that a friend passes you by without saying hello. If you had the thought, "Debra must be angry at me for doing something wrong," then you would likely feel *guilt*. If you had the thought, "Debra is trying to be mean and exclude me," you might feel *anger*. And, if you had the thought, "She didn't see me. That's just Debra. She always has her head in the clouds," then you may even feel some *amusement*. As shown in Figure 4.1,

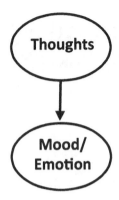

Figure 4.1

Part of the mood cycle: Thoughts can lead to a change in one's mood or emotions.

how you interpret or think about Debra's behavior directly affects how you feel (guilt vs. anger vs. amusement).

Behavior

Think of what your favorite activity is. Perhaps it's listening to your favorite music, going fishing or sailing, spending time with your loved ones, exercising, cooking your favorite meal, doing crafts, or hiking.

Think of what your least favorite activity is. Common examples are giving a presentation to a large audience, meeting deadlines at work, cleaning dishes after cooking a large meal, doing taxes, driving in traffic, and calling customer service.

Now imagine how you feel after doing your favorite activity versus how you feel after doing your least favorite activity. You should notice more positive emotions (e.g., joy, pride, excitement, energy) with your favorite activity and more negative emotions (e.g., anxiety, anger, frustration)

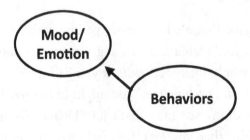

Figure 4.2

Part of the mood cycle: Behavior can lead to change in one's overall mood and emotions.

with your least favorite activity. As illustrated in Figure 4.2, what you do has a direct effect on how you feel.

Physical Sensations

Identify the emotions you feel when experiencing physical pain. You might feel anger, irritability, anxiety, sadness, or fear. Now identify the emotions you feel after feeling a release of muscle tension, which might make you feel relaxed, at ease, and content. Physical sensations also influence your emotions, as shown in Figure 4.3.

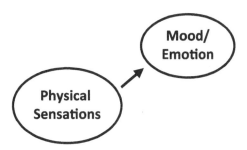

Figure 4.3

Part of the mood cycle: Physical sensations can lead to a change in one's mood or emotions.

Three Parts of Mood

Thoughts, behaviors, and physical sensations all affect your emotions. Emotions make up your mood. As shown in Figure 4.4, what you think, do, and feel physically affects your mood and can be thought of as parts of mood.

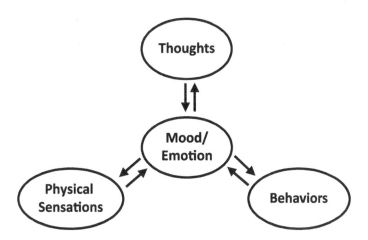

Figure 4.4

The mood cycle: Thoughts, physical sensations, and behaviors affect mood and vice versa.

The reverse is also true: Your mood and emotions affect what you think, do, and feel in your body. For example, feeling fear can lead you to think that you are in danger and make your heart race, and then you may run away. Feeling shame will result in thoughts of being "less than," urges to hide, and lowering your eyes or head. Feeling pride is likely to lead to thinking positively of yourself, being productive, and having an upright posture.

Further, as illustrated in Figure 4.5, each part of the mood triad affects other parts of mood—they are interconnected. How you *think* changes how you *feel* in your body and what you *do*. What you *do* changes how you *think* and what you *feel* in your body. And, what you *feel* changes what you *think* and do.

Most people seek therapy with the hope of turning off the way they feel, which is neither possible nor helpful. Imagine trying to shut off your depressed feelings or your racing heart like a light switch. You can't, and if you could, psychotherapy would not be needed. While we cannot and should not avoid feelings, we can change the way we think and behave, which in turn changes the way we feel. This is the cognitive–behavioral approach that the Positive Affect Treatment (PAT) uses. You will use a

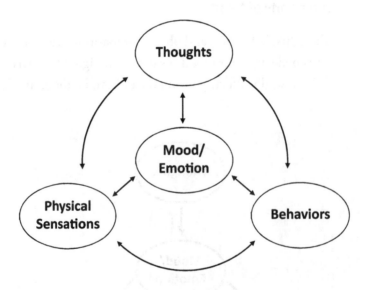

Figure 4.5

The mood cycle.

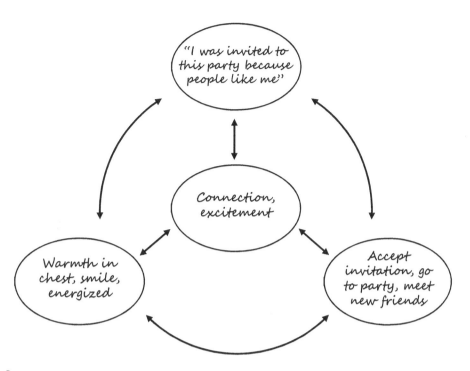

Figure 4.6

Felix's mood cycle.

combination of thinking skills and behavioral skills to improve your mood and increase the number, variety, and intensity of positive emotions. For example:

 Let's imagine Felix is invited to a party. As illustrated in Figure 4.6, if he has the thought that "I was invited to this party because people like me" (thought), Felix will likely notice a warmth in his chest and a smile on his face (physical sensations), as well as a feeling of connection (emotion). He may even feel more energized (physical sensation), will accept the invitation (behavior), feel excitement (emotion), and talk to people at the party (behavior), resulting in meeting a new friend.

Exercise 4.1: A Mood Cycle You Noticed

Your turn! Do you have a personal example like Felix's? Write it on Exercise 4.1: A Mood Cycle You Noticed. You may photocopy this exercise from the book or download multiple copies at the Treatments *That Work™* website (www.oxfordclinicalpsych.com/PAT).

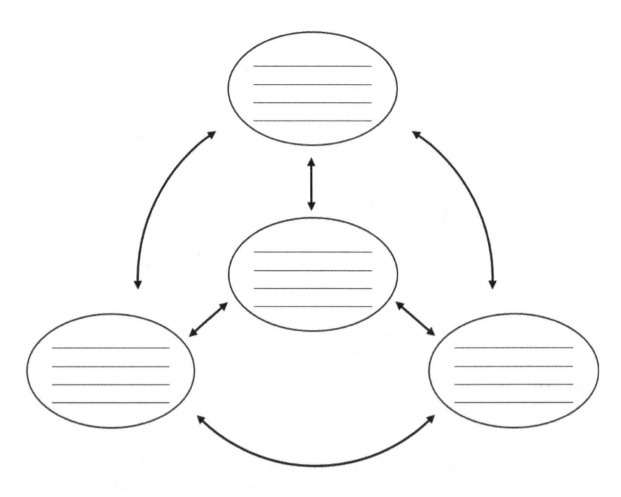

Exercise 4.1

A Mood Cycle You Noticed

Downward and Upward Spirals

Have you heard of downward spirals? An emotion (e.g., feeling down) leads to a negative thought (e.g., "I can't do anything right"), which leads to another negative thought (e.g., "I am an idiot and a failure"), which leads to more negative emotion (e.g., shame and more depression), which leads to a behavior (e.g., isolation), which only perpetuates the cycle. Downward spirals are examples of negative mood cycles, and as you may know, once you get in one, it's easy to get stuck in it.

The same is true of upward spirals. A positive thought (e.g., "I can do this") can lead to a positive emotion (e.g., confidence), which can lead to a behavior (e.g., being productive), which can lead to another positive thought (e.g., "I was successful") and emotion (e.g., pride), and so on. Upward spirals are a form of the mood cycle, but in the positive direction.

Science has shown that, like downward spirals, people can experience upward spirals, which are also self-perpetuating. Therefore, one of the goals of

PAT is to help you step into an upward spiral by changing your behavior and working with your thoughts. All of this is done through helpful figures and, of course, daily practice using the exercise forms. For example:

 Felix experienced an upward spiral when going for a walk (behavior). While walking around a nearby lake, he saw a couple of ducks with their newborn chicks following behind. Felix thought, "That's pretty neat" (thought). A small smile emerged (behavior) and he even started giggling (physical sensation) while watching the ducks. This led to an overall increase in his mood, especially in amusement and contentment (emotion), which led to feeling more motivation (emotion) to go on another walk. Indeed, the next day, Felix not only went for another walk (behavior), but he walked even farther.

Labeling Emotions

This treatment is uniquely designed to help you experience positive emotions again. To become aware of your positive emotions, it is crucial that you learn to label them. We cannot recognize and communicate our feel-

> **Labeling emotions** is intended to help with noticing positive experiences.

ings if we do not have words to describe them. *Labeling Emotions* allows us to both *notice* and *acknowledge* what we are feeling. Have you noticed that it is easy to find words that describe negative feelings and much harder to find words that describe positive feelings? It is important to expand your awareness and vocabulary of a variety of positive emotion labels in order to increase the accuracy and importance of what you are experiencing. As you move forward in this treatment, you will be completing exercises that prompt you to describe your positive emotions.

Examples of Positive Feeling Labels

Exercise 4.2: Positive Emotions Dial provides a set of labels for positive emotions. Read through the examples from Joy and Felix (on page 38), and on the Positive Emotions Dial form, identify the emotions that resonate most with you by placing an asterisk next to the word. Throughout this treatment, you will be recording the positive emotions you notice. This exercise form is meant to be a helpful reference when trying to identify those emotions. (Note: The type size of the labels does not indicate importance.) You may photocopy this exercise from the book or download multiple copies at the Treatments *That Work*™ website (www.oxfordclinicalpsych.com/PAT).

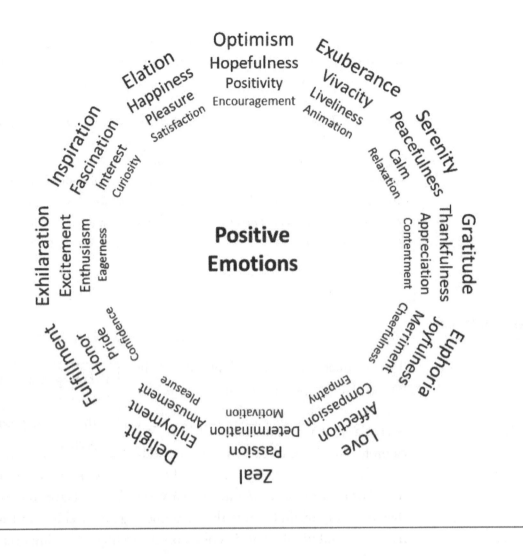

_____

_____

_____

_____

Exercise 4.2
Positive Emotions Dial

For homework, practice identifying and labeling positive emotions. On the blank lines, add additional positive emotions you might notice. You can refer back to and continue adding to the dial throughout treatment.

Examples from Joy and Felix

 Joy began reviewing the Positive Emotions Dial and realized that she was unaware that there were so many options for positive emotions. She also noticed that she hadn't experienced many positive emotions lately and tried hard to imagine every emotion listed.

She placed an asterisk next to respected, amused, proud, *and* thankful, *as those were the emotions that she missed the most.*

 Felix reviewed the Positive Emotions Dial and noticed that he had difficulty imagining some of the positive emotions listed. He placed asterisks next to curious, daring, *and* relaxed *because they stood out to him.*

Troubleshooting for Labeling Positive Emotions

Why Is Labeling Positive Emotions Important?

When we label emotions, we allow ourselves to notice and validate what we are experiencing at the moment. It is usually much easier for us to label our negative emotions and much more difficult to notice and label our positive emotions. Being able to acknowledge and label positive emotions expands our awareness of the various positive emotions available to us. It can also increase the accuracy of what we are feeling.

What If I Have a Hard Time Coming Up with New Positive Emotions?

That is completely normal and okay! It can be common for people with low mood to have a hard time generating positive emotions. This is why we provide you with the Positive Emotions Dial. If this exercise doesn't include the positive emotion you are experiencing, try your best to imagine past experiences or activities that you once enjoyed, and note the emotions you experience. The sooner you start to practice labeling positive emotions, the sooner you will be able to generate new positive emotions.

Treatment Skill Sets

CHAPTER 5 Actions Toward Feeling Better

The Function of Positive Activities

In this first treatment skill set, we are going to focus on behavior. As we discussed earlier, behavior is a part of your mood, and therefore, how you act directly affects how you feel and think. Low positive mood is often the result of not having enough positive activities in your life. (Remember the mood cycle? If not, go back to Chapter 4.) Behaviors such as social or emotional isolation, avoidance, and withdrawing contribute to maintaining low positive mood. Therefore, what do you think you have to do to jumpstart your mood? You have to change the way you behave! Why is this important to do? Research has shown that doing more activities overall (acting) usually leads to people feeling better and also leads to engaging in more rewarding activities. Being active promotes not only physical health but also mental health. "Feel better" behaviors or pleasurable activities typically lead to more positive thoughts and feelings. Have you ever heard the phrase "Fake it until you make it"? There is a lot of truth to that. Engaging in something is the best way to increase your mood, even if you may not feel motivated to do it.

You will further boost the pleasurable or rewarding activity by doing a detailed recounting with imagery. In addition, you will learn which pleasurable or rewarding activities will lead to positive feelings (learning), which will likely increase your motivation to engage in them (wanting) and your enjoyment of them (liking). You will also learn how to take steps toward doing those pleasurable activities.

Some people believe that they cannot enjoy activities because their low positive mood gets in the way. Therefore, they say, "What's the point?" and do not engage in positive activities. Or they say, "I don't deserve or have time to do fun things." Does that sound like you?

We will start by focusing on doing things that you currently find or have found positive at one time in your life. We will then work on deepening your experience of the positive aspects of those activities. Some people enjoy very few things due to their low positive mood, and therefore, they never engage in positive activities. Would you say that is a description of you?

As discussed, behavior is a part of the mood cycle; however, it is unique in that it is the element we can most directly influence. Unless restricted by a medical condition, we can move and be active no matter what we think or feel. On the contrary, we cannot easily shut off or turn on our thoughts, emotions, or physical sensations. Imagine you are sitting on the couch and have a water bottle sitting in front of you on the coffee table. Our minds can convince us that we are unable to get up and grab the bottle. How can it do that? Through feelings and thoughts. One of those feelings often reported in individuals who are depressed is that they lack energy. They feel heavy, unable to move. Their inner voice may say: "You are too tired to get up" or "What is the point in getting up? It won't change how you feel." However, unless you are paralyzed, you *can* get up, no matter how much your thoughts and feelings try to convince you that you cannot. If you get up and take that water bottle, your mind can no longer say you were unable to do it—because you just proved that you can.

> **Changing your behavior** is the most direct way of changing your thoughts and feelings.

Another important aspect of taking action is the first law of inertia. Do you remember it from middle school? "A body at rest will remain at rest, and a body in motion will remain in motion un-

> **Once in motion, it is easier to stay in motion.**

less it is acted upon by an external force." In other words, once you get moving, it will be easier to stay moving. For example, once you start taking a walk, it will be easier to keep walking, or once you start working on a task, it will be easier to keep working. The hardest part is often "getting in motion," otherwise known as getting started. It is not uncommon for individuals with depression and anhedonia to imagine something rewarding, but their motivation to get started is lacking. Make sure to keep this principle in mind for your assignments. It can "feel" overwhelming to get started, and your mind may tell you that it is pointless to do so. However, don't get tricked by that thought, and remember it is just that—a thought—not a fact. Tell yourself, "I don't know if it is pointless until I do it."

Monitoring Daily Activities and Mood

We will begin monitoring your activity level. Why is this important? Knowing why something is important increases the likelihood that you will complete the activity. If you know that sitting on the couch has the same effect on your mood and body as exercise, would you exercise? Probably not. Here are the reasons that monitoring activity is so important:

1. It informs you where your starting point is, which is essential for monitoring progress.
2. It creates an objective and accurate representation of your daily activities.
3. It shows you where you may have some more time for positive activities.
4. It shows you the relationship between the activity and mood.

Refer to Exercise 5.1: Daily Activity and Mood Record, on page 47. Monitoring includes recording the number of hours you sleep, how much you engage in physical activities, the number of hours you spend online, the number of activities you complete, and so on. You may be surprised at the difference between what you think you are doing during the day and what you are actually doing. Figure 5.1 is an example completed by Felix.

Daily Activity and Mood Record

Instructions:
Monitor and record your daily activities throughout the day. Be sure to rate your mood before and after each activity (0=lowest mood, 10=highest mood). Try to record your activities every day this week. Use a different Daily Activity and Mood Record for each day.

Day of the Week: _Tuesday_

	Activity	Mood Before (0-10)	Mood After (0-10)
1:00	sleep		
2:00	sleep		
3:00	sleep		
4:00	sleep		
5:00	sleep		
6:00	sleep		
7:00	sleep		
8:00	sleep		3
9:00	Check phone in bed	3	2
10:00	Play videogames	2	
11:00	Watch tv		3
12:00	Eat lunch	4	4
13:00	Talk on phone with mom	4	7
14:00	Play videogames	6	
15:00	Play videogames		
16:00	Watch tv		
17:00	Play videogames		
18:00	Play videogames		1
19:00	Eat dinner	3	3
20:00	Watch tv	3	3
21:00	Browse internet	3	
22:00	Browse internet		
23:00	Browse internet		2
24:00	sleep	2	

Figure 5.1

Felix's completed Daily Activity and Mood Record.

Exercise 5.1: Daily Activity and Mood Record

Now it's your turn! Over the next seven days, complete a Daily Activity and Mood Record (Exercise 5.1) at the end of each day. You may photocopy this exercise from the book or download multiple copies at the Treatments *That Work*™ website (www.oxfordclinicalpsych.com/PAT).

As you keep track of activities, also monitor your mood after each activity. For example, notice what your mood is like following a dinner

Daily Activity and Mood Record

Instructions:

Monitor and record your daily activities throughout the day. Be sure to rate your mood before and after each activity (0=lowest mood, 10=highest mood). Try to record your activities every day this week. Use a different Daily Activity and Mood Record for each day.

Day of the Week: _____

	Activity	Mood Before (0-10)	Mood After (0-10)
1.00			
2.00			
3.00			
4.00			
5.00			
6.00			
7.00			
8.00			
9.00			
10.00			
11.00			
12.00			
13.00			
14.00			
15.00			
16.00			
17.00			
18.00			
19.00			
20.00			
21.00			
22.00			
23.00			
24.00			

Exercise 5.1

Daily Activity and Mood Record

with friends versus after watching TV. Why is this important? Because the purpose of this part of the treatment is to use behavior to increase your positive mood. You won't know if you are increasing your mood if you don't track it. This is similar to other things we may try to track in order to manage it (e.g., our weight, health, finances). It's challenging to manage what we don't measure. Plus, you may learn that certain activities are closely tied to positive mood for you, while others are not. Monitoring helps with learning that connection.

Designing Positive Activities

Over the next few weeks, we will increase the positive activities you engage in. Both designing and practicing positive activities can lead to an increase in positive emotions. First, let's start by focusing on things that you currently find positive, once found positive, or think could be positive if you try them.

Exercise 5.2: Positive Activity List and Exercise 5.3: Positive Activity List Through Mastery

Look at Exercise 5.2: Positive Activity List, and identify whether each activity is a *current* activity that brings you positive emotions, a *past* activity that brought on positive emotions, or a new activity that you can *try*. Identify and label the positive activities that you currently do with a "C," those you have done in the past with a "P," and those you would like to try with a "T." Using the extra lines, add any other activities you currently enjoy, have enjoyed, or think you might enjoy. Then review Exercise 5.3: Positive Activity List Through Mastery, using the same labels ("C," "P," and "T"). Add any additional activities that currently bring on a feeling of mastery or that might bring on that feeling. You may photocopy these exercises from the book or download multiple copies at the Treatments *That Work*™ website (www.oxfordclinicalpsych. com/PAT).

Positive Activity List

Instructions: Review the list of positive activities. Identify whether each activity is a *current* activity that brings you positive emotions, a *past* activity that brought on positive emotions, or a new activity that you can *try.* Label each positive activity with C for current, P for past, or T for trying something new. Add any additional activities that you currently enjoy, have enjoyed, or think you might enjoy.

C, P, T _____

_____ Taking a bath

_____ Going to a concert

_____ Going to a sports event

_____ Having lunch with friends or colleagues

_____ Going to bar, tavern, club, etc.

_____ Reading a book for pleasure

_____ Playing with animals

_____ Spending time in nature

_____ Watching a movie, series, or sports

_____ Going to a party

_____ Hanging out with friends

_____ Cooking

_____ Thinking about a positive future

_____ Enjoying a favorite snack

_____ Cuddling with a significant other

_____ Exercising, hiking, or playing sports

_____ Exploring (e.g., going a new route)

_____ Putting on makeup, doing my hair, etc.

_____ Dressing up in nice clothes

_____ Going to the movie theater

_____ Watching funny movies or clips

_____ Getting a massage

_____ _____

_____ _____

C, P, T _____

_____ Buying things for myself

_____ Going to religious or community functions

_____ Going to class or club event

_____ Buying a gift for family or friends

_____ Donating to charity or volunteering

_____ Making food or crafts to give away

_____ Dancing to my favorite song

_____ Catching up with a friend

_____ Being with children or grandchildren

_____ Helping others

_____ Breathing fresh air

_____ Playing video games with friends

_____ Playing a musical instrument

_____ Doing artwork (e.g., painting, photography)

_____ Smelling my favorite candle scent

_____ Playing cards or board games

_____ Going on a walk

_____ Writing a letter

_____ Looking at pictures

_____ Gardening

_____ Getting a manicure or pedicure

_____ _____

_____ _____

Exercise 5.2

Positive Activity List

Positive Activity List through Mastery

Instructions: Review the list of positive activities that build mastery. Identify whether each activity is a *current* activity that you are practicing, a *past* activity, or a new activity that you can *try*. Label each activity with C for current, P for past, or T for trying something new. Add any additional activities that currently bring on a feeling of mastery or that might bring on that feeling.

C, P, T

_____ Working towards meeting a deadline

_____ Learning a new skill (e.g., language)

_____ Finishing a project

_____ Cleaning the dishes

_____ Vacuuming

_____ Organizing

_____ Planning trips or vacations

_____ Studying for an exam

_____ Working on a jigsaw puzzle

_____ _____

_____ _____

C, P, T

_____ Learning a musical instrument

_____ Reading a book

_____ Writing stories, novels, plays, or poetry

_____ Learning a new hobby (e.g., craft)

_____ Redecorating a room

_____ Working on an application

_____ Restoring furniture or antiques

_____ Arranging songs or music

_____ Completing homework

_____ _____

_____ _____

Exercise 5.3

Positive Activity List Through Mastery

Exercise 5.4: My Positive Activity List

Now it's your turn! Using Exercise 5.4: My Positive Activity List, create a list of: (1) activities that you currently find enjoyable, once found enjoyable, or believe that you could find enjoyable, (2) activities that bring value to your life, and (3) activities that may not bring immediate enjoyment but produce feelings of mastery (or other positive emotions) following their completion. You may photocopy this exercise from the book or download multiple copies at the Treatments *That Work*™ website (www.oxfordclinicalpsych.com/PAT).

You can start with the positive activities you already engage in. If you have trouble coming up with examples, remind yourself of the activities you liked on the earlier lists. In addition to listing activities that you find positive and enjoyable, list activities that bring value to your life, such as helping a friend or improving your health. Also, make sure to include activities that may not bring immediate enjoyment or reward but produce feelings of mastery (or other positive emotions) when you have done them.

As you list the positive activities, think about the last time you engaged in this activity and why you are currently not engaging in it. Then, rate the level of difficulty (0 = easy and 10 = most difficult) for you to complete

My Positive Activity List

Record: (1) activities that you currently find enjoyable, once found enjoyable, or believe that you could find enjoyable, (2) activities that bring value to your life, and (3) activities that may not bring immediate enjoyment but produce feelings of mastery (or other positive emotions) following their completion. Rate the level of difficulty (0 – easy, 10 – most difficult) for you to complete each item.

Activity	Difficulty (0-10)
1. Having lunch with my daughter	6
2. Watching the sunset	2
3. Going on a run	4
4. Watching my favorite movie	3
5. Helping my elderly neighbor	9
6. Having coffee with a friend	7
7. Trying a yoga class	10
8. Cleaning the house	6
9. Meeting a work deadline	8
10. Having friends over for dinner	7

Figure 5.2

Joy's My Positive Activity List.

each activity. We want to make sure you are beginning with activities that you find more manageable.

Note that it is important to have a range of activities, and some should involve other people. Some should be shorter in duration, and others should be longer. For example, eating your favorite food can be a positive activity, but it may elicit less positive emotion than spending an afternoon with a friend. Figure 5.2 is an example from Joy's My Positive Activity List and Figure 5.3 is an example from Felix's list.

"Feel better" behaviors or pleasurable activities promote mental and physical health as they lead to more positive thoughts and feelings.

My Positive Activity List

Record: (1) activities that you currently find enjoyable, once found enjoyable, or believe that you could find enjoyable, (2) activities that bring value to your life, and (3) activities that may not bring immediate enjoyment but produce feelings of mastery (or other positive emotions) following their completion. Rate the level of difficulty (0 – easy, 10 – most difficult) for you to complete each item.

Activity	Difficulty (0-10)
1. Calling a friend	6
2. Playing video games	2
3. Volunteering at the local church	10
4. Going to the fitness studio	8
5. Taking a morning walk	6
6. Applying for a new job	9
7. Having dinner with a friend	8
8. Getting outside for fresh air	3
9. Buying groceries	5
10. Exploring a new neighborhood	7

Figure 5.3

Felix's My Positive Activity List.

My Positive Activity List

Record: (1) activities that you currently find enjoyable, once found enjoyable, or believe that you could find enjoyable, (2) activities that bring value to your life, and (3) activities that may not bring immediate enjoyment but produce feelings of mastery (or other positive emotions) following their completion. Rate the level of difficulty (0 – easy, 10 – most difficult) for you to complete each item.

Activity	Difficulty (0–10)
1. _____	_____
2. _____	_____
3. _____	_____
4. _____	_____
5. _____	_____
6. _____	_____
7. _____	_____
8. _____	_____
9. _____	_____
10. _____	_____

Exercise 5.4

My Positive Activity List

Troubleshooting for Designing Positive Activities

What Do I Do If None of the Items on the Positive Activity List Interest Me?

You might think that none of the examples on the Positive Activity List in Exercise 5.2 will interest you. This is likely a symptom of anhedonia. Even though it may be difficult to believe that any of the activities would spark some positive emotions for you, science suggests that doing the activities suggested on the list or your own will generate positive emotion for you. Therefore, we suggest that you try at least one activity and observe whether positive emotions arise before, during, or after that activity. If no positive emotions arise, try several other activities.

Well done! You have completed the My Positive Activity List (Exercise 5.4) and your Daily Activity and Mood Record (Exercise 5.1). How many positive activities did you do last week? How much did you enjoy them? Did they improve your mood?

We will use this information for our next exercise, Positive Activity Scheduling (see Exercise 5.5 on page 58). What is that? Over the following weeks, you will work on introducing more and more rewarding activities into your daily routine. Those can include activities you already do—those listed on your Daily Activity and Mood Record—or new ones, such as activities that you enjoyed in the past or always wanted to try out. As mentioned earlier, it is also important to include activities that may not feel or look very rewarding right away—such as cleaning the house or completing a deadline—but give you a sense of mastery, ownership, or accomplishment when you have done them.

Here is an example for Joy (Figure 5.4):

Joy initially found it difficult to think about activities that she currently enjoys. After giving it some thought, she realized that she missed spending time with her friends, and she decided to invite her friend Sam for dinner (category "social" and "leisure"). Joy wrote down the necessary steps to make the activity more manageable to follow through with it. She wrote, "Call Sam to coordinate time," and then "Find recipes," and then "Prep food" and "Cook." She also specified how often she would do the activity (one time this week), the day/time/duration (Friday evening), and who would be involved (Sam). She recorded her mood before and after dinner with Sam (e.g., from a 3 out of 10 to an 8 out of 10) on her Positive Activity Scheduling exercise sheet. She noticed that her mood improved and that she felt cheerful, connected, and proud.

Here is an example for Felix (Figure 5.5):

Felix began thinking about activities that he used to enjoy. He remembered that he used to like going for walks outside and decided that he would begin walking for 15 minutes each morning (category "health" and "leisure"). The steps required to complete the exercise were, "Set alarm for 8:30am," "Find a playlist," "Have a cup of coffee," and "Put on workout clothes." Felix recorded his mood before and after the walk each day (e.g., from a 3 out of 10 to a 5 out of 10) on his Positive Activity Scheduling exercise sheet, and noticed that his mood improved. He also noticed that he felt accomplished and energized.

Positive Activity Scheduling

Instructions:

Identify one new activity from your Positive Activity List that you can engage in this week. Write this activity in the Activity box. Identify which category (e.g., social, work, health, leisure, spirituality, other) the activity falls into. If your activity requires steps to complete it, enter those steps in the How to Complete Activity box. Rate the difficulty level of each step on a 0-10 scale (0=least difficult, 10=most difficult). Then complete the paragraph, filling in the number of times in the week, the days in the week, time of day, the duration, and who you might be doing the activity with. Then, practice the activity throughout the week, recording your mood before and after on a 0-10 scale (0=lowest mood, 10=highest mood). Also, record any positive emotions you may have noticed before, during, or after engaging in the activity.

Activity

Invite Sam for dinner

Category

- ☒ Social
- ☐ Work
- ☐ Health
- ☒ Leisure
- ☐ Spirituality
- ☐ Other

How to Complete Activity

Steps	Difficulty (0-10)
1. Call Sam to coordinate time	6
2. Find recipes	3
3. Prep food	5
4. Cook	8
5. Have Sam over	6
6.	
7.	
8.	

For homework, I will complete this activity __1__ times this week, on ___Friday___ (M, Tu, W, etc.) in the ___evening___ (morning, afternoon, evening) for __2 hrs__ (# of: sec, min, hrs) with ___Sam___ (name; if applicable).

Homework #	Mood Before (0-10)	Mood After (0-10)	Positive Emotion(s)
1	3	8	Cheerful, connected, proud
2			
3			
4			
5			
6			
7			

Figure 5.4

Joy's completed Positive Activity Scheduling sheet. Note that Joy only had to record her mood once since she only did the activity one time. For an activity that is done several times a week, such as running, she would rate the mood every time she does it (see the example from Felix in Figure 5.5).

Positive Activity Scheduling

Instructions:

Identify one new activity from your Positive Activity List that you can engage in this week. Write this activity in the Activity box. Identify which category (e.g., social, work, health, leisure, spirituality, other) the activity falls into. If your activity requires steps to complete it, enter those steps in the How to Complete Activity box. Rate the difficulty level of each step on a 0-10 scale (0=least difficult, 10=most difficult). Then complete the paragraph, filling in the number of times in the week, the days in the week, time of day, the duration, and who you might be doing the activity with. Then, practice the activity throughout the week, recording your mood before and after on a 0-10 scale (0=lowest mood, 10=highest mood). Also, record any positive emotions you may have noticed before, during, or after engaging in the activity.

Activity

Go for 15 minute walk

Category

- ☐ Social
- ☐ Work
- ☒ Health
- ☒ Leisure
- ☐ Spirituality
- ☐ Other

How to Complete Activity

Steps	Difficulty (0-10)
1. *Set alarm for 8:30am*	6
2. *Find a playlist*	2
3. *Have a cup of coffee*	2
4. *Put on workout clothes*	4
5. *Go for walk*	8
6.	
7.	
8.	

For homework, I will complete this activity __7__ times this week, on ___*everyday*___ (M, Tu, W, etc.) in the ___*morning*___ (morning, afternoon, evening) for ___*15 mins*___ (# of: sec, min, hrs) with ___*by myself*___ (name; if applicable).

Homework #	Mood Before (0-10)	Mood After (0-10)	Positive Emotion(s)
1	3	5	*accomplished*
2	1	4	*hopeful*
3	2	6	*energized*
4	4	5	*proud*
5	3	7	*inspired*
6	5	6	*strong*
7	2	5	*refreshed*

Figure 5.5

Felix's completed Positive Activity Scheduling sheet.

Now it's time for the fun! Choose an activity from your My Positive Activity List (Exercise 5.4), and write it down on Exercise 5.5: Positive Activity Scheduling. Note that some activities require multiple steps; in this case, list each individual step on Exercise 5.5 rather than lumping together the entire task. Use one copy of Exercise 5.5 per positive activity. You may photocopy this exercise from the book or download multiple copies at the Treatments *That Work*™ website (www.oxfordclinicalpsych.com/PAT).

Writing out the necessary steps will help you make the activities more manageable. Even fun activities sometimes require a bit of planning and work. By starting with easier activities and anticipating obstacles, you will increase the chances of completing them. Lastly, decide which category your activity best falls into (e.g., social, work, health). If you notice that most of your activities fall into only one category, try to mix it up. Having at least some social activities is strongly encouraged.

Record your mood from 0 (lowest mood) to 10 (highest mood) before and after the activity. Also, record the positive emotion you experience either before, during, or after the activity. Make sure to refer back to Exercise 4.2: Positive Emotions Dial from chapter 4.

For your weekly homework, choose three to five new activities from Exercise 5.4. Using one Positive Activity Scheduling sheet per activity, start with the easiest few activities, and then work your way up. Make sure to break the activities down into steps if needed.

Positive Activity Scheduling

Instructions:
Identify one new activity from your Positive Activity List that you can engage in this week. Write this activity in the Activity box. Identify which category (e.g., social, work, health, leisure, spirituality, other) the activity falls into. If your activity requires steps to complete it, enter those steps in the How to Complete Activity box. Rate the difficulty level of each step on a 0-10 scale (0=least difficult, 10=most difficult). Then complete the paragraph, filling in the number of times in the week, the days in the week, time of day, the duration, and who you might be doing the activity with. Then, practice the activity throughout the week, recording your mood before and after on a 0-10 scale (0=lowest mood, 10=highest mood). Also, record any positive emotions you may have noticed before, during, or after engaging in the activity.

Activity

Category

- ☐ Social ☐ Leisure
- ☐ Work ☐ Spirituality
- ☐ Health ☐ Other

How to Complete Activity

Steps	Difficulty (0-10)
1. _____	_____
2. _____	_____
3. _____	_____
4. _____	_____
5. _____	_____
6. _____	_____
7. _____	_____
8. _____	_____

For homework, I will complete this activity _____ times this week, on _____ (M, Tu, W, etc.) in the _____ (morning, afternoon, evening) for _____ (# of: sec, min, hrs) with _____ (name; if applicable).

Homework #	Mood Before (0-10)	Mood After (0-10)	Positive Emotion(s)
1			
2			
3			
4			
5			
6			
7			

Exercise 5.5

Positive Activity Scheduling

Troubleshooting for Practicing Positive Activities

What If I Don't Feel Like Doing This?

Remember that lack of motivation is a symptom of anhedonia but also anxiety, depression, and stress. If you would feel like doing positive activities— you would already be doing them! Unfortunately, the less we do, the harder it becomes. Remember the first law of inertia? If you stay inactive, it is much harder to become active than when you are already active! This is why it is easier to keep running than to start running. Likewise, have you ever heard the phrase "Fake it until you make it"? There is a lot of truth to that phrase. Engaging in something you may not feel motivated to do nor want to do is the best way to increase your mood.

I Have a Hard Time Engaging in Positive Events

This makes sense. A lot of people with anhedonia struggle with exactly this. We recommend that you try the following. First write down the barrier to the specific event. Then check to see if it matches any of the following:

It's too difficult: If the barrier is that the activity is too difficult, break it up into it smaller, more manageable steps. Or just choose a simpler activity to start with.

It's too scary: If the barrier is fear that the activity won't be pleasurable, ask yourself if there is any evidence to support that fear. If there is no evidence, ask yourself if you would be willing to test out whether the activity would be pleasurable. Make sure you notice your mood before and after engaging in the activity.

It doesn't improve my mood: If there is evidence from past attempts that the activity did not increase your mood, (1) choose another activity, (2) think about why the activity was not pleasurable, or (3) ask yourself whether you would be willing to retest how pleasurable the activity is.

I can't get motivated to do it: If the problem is a lack of motivation, remind yourself about the reason why positive events scheduling is helpful to improve your mood. Ask yourself the following questions: "What is the benefit of doing things I find pleasurable?" and "How has not engaging in pleasurable activities been working for me?" Make a list of pros and cons of engaging in positive events.

I don't feel better afterward: Have you noticed that your mind wanders or you get distracted during the exercise? If so, you are unlikely to notice positive consequences of positive events scheduling. Try to remain "in the moment" (i.e., mindful) during the positive activities. Also, try not to be too harsh on yourself. Be compassionate and remind yourself that changing behaviors is difficult and takes time and practice.

Until now, we have focused on improving the "wanting" and "liking." In the next step, we also want to improve the "learning." What does this mean, and how will we do that? Let's use an example: Imagine your positive activity was to visit your daughter. As instructed, you broke down the activity into multiple, manageable steps, such as calling her to arrange the dates, booking your flights and hotel, making reservations for a nice meal together, and packing your bags. You rated your mood before and after the event and noticed an increase in your positive mood.

Let's do a time warp! In your mind, go back to the event and zoom in to a particularly positive and rewarding moment (e.g., the moment your daughter picked you up from the airport). Recount this moment in the present tense! You can do that by writing it down (see Figure 5.6 for an example) or saying it silently to yourself or aloud with your eyes closed. You can even record it. Make sure to stay in the present moment and try to really focus on what you are experiencing. A good way to do this is to focus

---

Savoring the Moment

Instructions: Identify and record a positive activity or event from this week. Recount the event in your mind, visualizing what you saw, heard, felt, thought, smelled, and tasted. Record your level of mood (0=lowest mood, 10=highest mood) before and after the recounting, as well as the vividness of the recounting (10=most vivid). Also, identify any positive emotions you noticed, in addition to any other reactions (e.g., thoughts, physical sensations).

Event	Mood Before (0-10)	Mood After (0-10)	Vividness (0-10)	Positive Emotion(s)	Reactions (thoughts, physical sensations)
In the car with my daughter	4	7	8	Love, pride	Warmth, smile, "I love my daughter"
Dinner with Sam	2	4	6	Connected, amused	Giggling, "Sam can be funny"

Figure 5.6

Illustration of a *Savoring the Moment* activity for Joy.

on your sensory experience—what did you feel? Hear? Taste? How vividly can you imagine the event? We call this exercise *Savoring the Moment*.

Why is *Savoring the Moment* important to do? Savoring a rewarding experience deepens your appreciation of the activity or event; it also deepens your experience of the positive aspects of the activity and the emotions you felt, which you might otherwise have ignored or dismissed. By recounting the memory, particularly the most positive aspects of the activity, you are re-experiencing those positive aspects and strengthening the learning between activity and mood. In turn, that learning increases interest and preference for other positive experiences over negative experiences, all of which increases positive emotions and future involvement in positive activities.

Research has shown that we are more likely to do things that are positively reinforced (rewarding). To find them rewarding, we need to do them again and again and remind ourselves what was rewarding about them. Unfortunately, when our mood is low, our brain tends to focus on and remember the negative aspects of even positive events. Through *Savoring the Moment* exercises, we can deepen the experience of positive emotions. Thus, a "savoring" recounting helps us savor pleasurable moments and enhance their short-term and long-term impact by creating a stronger connection between our behavioral accomplishments and mood. We will deepen our learning on which of our actions leads to positive emotions.

Exercise 5.6: Savoring the Moment

Your turn! At the end of each week, choose one or two of the activities you did and practice *Savoring the Moment* by completing Exercise 5.6. You may photocopy this exercise from the book or download multiple copies at the Treatments *That Work*™ website (www.oxfordclinicalpsych. com/PAT). This exercise needs to be as detailed as possible and should include the thoughts, emotions, and physical sensations that you experienced during the activity. We recommend closing your eyes and thinking about the activity first. Then describe in the present tense the positive aspects of the experience in detail. Be sure to use the following questions:

- How did you know you were experiencing a positive emotion?
- What specific physical sensations did you have?

- What specific thoughts did you have?
- What positive emotions did you experience?
- What was your mood before and after the experience?
- What did you learn about how your mood and the activity are related?
- How did recounting the experience influence your mood?
- What is your mood after writing about the experience on a scale of 0 to 10? Did your mood change?

We encourage you to informally practice *Savoring the Moment* after a pleasurable activity to further strengthen "learning" of what actions lead to positive feelings.

Savoring the Moment

Instructions: Identify and record a positive activity or event from this week. Recount the event in your mind, visualizing what you saw, heard, felt, thought, smelled, and tasted. Record your level of mood (0=lowest mood, 10=highest mood) before and after the recounting, as well as the vividness of the recounting (10=most vivid). Also, identify any positive emotions you noticed, in addition to any other reactions (e.g., thoughts, physical sensations).

Event	Mood Before (0-10)	Mood After (0-10)	Vividness (0-10)	Positive Emotion(s)	Reactions (thoughts, physical sensations)

Exercise 5.6

Savoring the Moment

Troubleshooting for Savoring the Moment

How Does Savoring the Moment Help Me?

By recounting the memory in depth, you are re-experiencing the positive aspects of the activity and strengthening the learning between activity and mood. This will help you remember those moments better and therefore feel more interested in those activities.

Why Can't I Stay in the Moment?

It can be difficult to stay focused, especially when you find yourself worrying about past or future events. Just like in yoga or meditation, it can be challenging to stay in the moment. Expect to get distracted or maybe even a bit frustrated at first. Try to slow down and really visualize what you are feeling. Keep your recounting in the present tense and try to use as many positive words from the Positive Emotions Dial (Exercise 4.2). It can help to purposefully smile, close your eyes, uncross your arms, or open your hands. This change in body language can help you stay in the moment and connect better to your positive emotions. As with any skill, continued practice will lead to mastery. Remember to focus on how the positive experience makes you feel, think, and act, and try to describe those experiences in detail. Ask yourself how you know that you are experiencing a positive emotion.

CHAPTER 6

Attending to the Positive

The Function of Attending to the Positive

In the second treatment skill set, you are going to work with your thoughts. The focus here is to increase your ability to imagine positive outcomes, notice and appreciate the positive, and learn how your behaviors can lead to positive outcomes. Remember the mood cycle we discussed in chapter 4? Behaviors, thoughts, and feelings are all connected. After spending the past several weeks working on changing your behavior, now it's time to focus on your thoughts! Our thoughts, beliefs, and interpretations of situations influence how we *feel*. Here is an example:

 Joy receives an email from her boss asking her to come to her office. She interprets this email as an indication that her boss will:

1. *fire her*
2. *praise her*
3. *give her a raise*
4. *criticize her work*

Did you select one of the negative options? If so, that's okay! Your mind has likely drifted toward negative assumptions for a long time. We are going to work on changing that.

Which of the following emotions would follow each of these interpretations?

1. proud
2. anxious
3. happy
4. angry

Do you notice how the negative interpretations lead to negative emotions and positive interpretations lead to positive emotions? In this skill set, you will start to shift your mind toward the positive direction to increase the number of positive emotions you experience.

The next set of skills that you learn will increase your positive thinking in a more balanced way. The more positive we think, the more positive we feel. The skills you learn will help you recognize positive aspects that already exist.

Overview of Attending to the Positive

Some people have difficulty noticing and appreciating positive events when they occur. Do you ever find yourself saying that good things never happen to you? When a positive event does happen, do you dismiss it, or maybe not even notice it? For example, if you receive a compliment, do you dismiss it as not genuine? Or do you dismiss your own achievements and instead focus on your failures? If you find that this is characteristic of you, you will most likely have difficulty noticing or appreciating the positive.

Also, some people have difficulty taking ownership of positive events. Do you ever notice yourself assuming that it must have been someone or something else (e.g., luck) that caused a positive outcome to occur, and not you yourself? Maybe you believe other people are the reason for good things happening to you. When was the last time you took credit for a positive event that you contributed to ? This treatment program will help you start attending to the positive and then taking ownership of it.

Additionally, you may fail to imagine or anticipate that a positive event will occur in the future. People with anhedonia tend to do that more often than others. Do you notice yourself imagining mostly negative events in the future? How does that make you feel?

In this part of the treatment, you will practice noticing and appreciating the positive (liking) in events that have happened (using the skills of *Finding the Silver Linings* and *Taking Ownership*), as well as learning the connection between your efforts and positive outcomes (learning) (*Taking Ownership*). You will also practice imagining good things happening in the future (wanting) (*Imagining the Positive*).

Our brains are like muscles. The more we use them, the better they become at doing certain things. This means that—like a muscle—we can train or strengthen our brains to do certain things. During this part of treatment, you will begin to train your mind to attend to the positive.

How do you strengthen a muscle? Yes, through exercise! Exercise is a type of practice. The more you do it, the stronger your muscle becomes. Will your muscles get stronger if you only lift weights once a year? Once a month? Once a week? What about daily? If you want to train your brain to attend to the positive, you need to practice multiple times per week.

How do you attend to the positive? After some basic education on certain thinking traps people with anhedonia fall into, you will learn three different strategies to help shift your attention toward the positive:

- A common thinking trap among people with anhedonia is failing to recognize the positive when present. Therefore, you will learn how to find the silver linings in events. That means that you will practice identifying at least one positive aspect in past and present situations.
- Another common thinking trap is not taking ownership of positive events. You will practice listing ways you have contributed to something going well.
- The third thinking trap is assuming future events will turn out negatively. To target this, you will practice imagining future events more positively.

Some people with anhedonia believe that if they focus too much on the positive, they will not be able to prepare for the negative. Although this program does not target negative thoughts directly, our research has shown that it does so indirectly by boosting your positive thinking.

Further, in this treatment, we emphasize that planning for the future is important. However, when thoughts about the future become worries that interfere with an ability to have a balanced view of the future, it becomes problematic. In the Positive Affect Treatment (PAT) program, you are building your muscle toward thinking more positively so that your thoughts overall become more balanced (instead of more negative).

"Every cloud has a silver lining" is a saying that suggests there is something positive in every situation. Believing that there is a silver lining in most situations can feel too optimistic and unrealistic to many people. This is a common belief among people with anhedonia. The unfamiliar often feels strange at first, and it can be difficult to believe that a new way of thinking can be helpful. However, with practice, this new way of thinking will become more natural, and old thinking traps (e.g., difficulty noticing the positive) will lessen.

> **Noticing** and **appreciating** positive aspects of events and everyday things boosts positive emotions.

Finding the Silver Linings means finding at least one positive aspect of a given event. By starting to recognize silver linings, our brains learn that most events have something positive about them and some events may even be mostly positive.

Since we are building the positivity muscle, you will be identifying more than one silver lining in each exercise. (See Exercise 6.1: Finding the Silver Linings on page 72). This is part of strengthening the skill. Like when you're strengthening a muscle, you have to exercise attending to the positive more intensely during the learning stage. It is just like having to exercise more frequently and intensely when trying to build strength. But once your strength is established, you don't have to maintain such an intense exercise program.

Here is an example from Felix:

 Yesterday, Felix's friend Bobbi helped him with the résumé that Felix created to submit with job applications. Working on his résumé was one of Felix's activities intended to improve his sense of mastery. The document was covered in red ink with Bobbi's corrections, and they spent an hour going over formatting and content revisions. What can Felix think of as silver linings from this event? In other words, what are some positive aspects of this event? Here are some possibilities:

- *Felix now knows better how to write and format a résumé.*
- *He also had a productive conversation with his friend.*
- *Bobbi took the time to give feedback, a sign that Bobbi wants Felix to succeed.*

- *Felix is now one step closer to sending in job applications.*
- *His mood improved, and Felix feels productive and proud.*

Figure 6.1 shows an example of Felix's completed *Finding the Silver Linings* exercise sheet.

Finding the Silver Linings

Instructions: Record the date of your practice. Then identify and record a positive, negative, or neutral situation. Identify as many positive aspects (at least 6) of that situation, and write them down under Silver Linings. Don't forget to write down your mood before and after the exercise on a 0-10 scale (0=lowest mood, 10=highest mood). Also, write down any positive emotions you experienced before, during, or after the exercise. Try to complete one exercise a day.

Practice Date: *October 10, 4pm*

Situation: *I received several edits on my resumé that I had been writing*

Silver Linings:

1. *I now know how to write a resumé*
2. *It was a helpful conversation*
3. *I learned a lot*
4. *Bobbi cares enough to take time for feedback*
5. *I know how to format a resumé*
6. *I am closer to getting a job*

Mood Before (0-10)	Mood After (0-10)	Positive Emotion(s)
2	5	*Productive, pride*

Figure 6.1

Felix's completed *Finding the Silver Linings* exercise.

Here is an example from Joy:

 Several days ago, Joy and her husband invited a couple over for dinner at their house. This was one of Joy's positive activities intended to improve her mood because she used to really enjoy hosting dinner parties in the past. This time, the main course was overcooked, and there was a lot of noise from a gathering at her neighbor's home. Joy could have focused on those negative elements and completely ignored the positives. What can Joy think of as silver linings from this event? Here are some possibilities:

- *Joy saw her friends, whom she hasn't seen in a long time.*
- *Joy learned how to cook a new recipe and how to improve it in the future.*
- *Her friends seemed to enjoy themselves and so did she.*
- *She felt good about accomplishing a goal she had set for herself.*

Figure 6.2 illustrates an example of Joy's completed *Finding the Silver Linings* exercise sheet.

Finding the Silver Linings

Instructions: Record the date of your practice. Then identify and record a positive, negative, or neutral situation. Identify as many positive aspects (at least 6) of that situation, and write them down under Silver Linings. Don't forget to write down your mood before and after the exercise on a 0-10 scale (0=lowest mood, 10=highest mood). Also, write down any positive emotions you experienced before, during, or after the exercise. Try to complete one exercise a day.

Practice Date: _June 14th, 8pm_

Situation: _I invited my friends over for dinner, and I overcooked the main course_

Silver Linings:

1. _I got to see my friends that I haven't seen in a while_
2. _I learned how to cook a new recipe_
3. _I know what mistakes not to make next time_
4. _My friends seemed to enjoy themselves_
5. _I laughed more than I have in a while_
6. _I accomplished my goal of having friends over_

Mood Before (0-10)	Mood After (0-10)	Positive Emotion(s)
5	7	Joy, pride, connected

Figure 6.2

Joy's completed *Finding the Silver Linings* exercise.

Exercise 6.1: Finding the Silver Linings

Now it's your turn! Using Exercise 6.1: Finding the Silver Linings, complete the form with an example from your week. Take a situation that felt

---

Finding the Silver Linings

Instructions: Record the date of your practice. Then identify and record a positive, negative, or neutral situation. Identify as many positive aspects (at least 6) of that situation, and write them down under Silver Linings. Don't forget to write down your mood before and after the exercise on a 0-10 scale (0=lowest mood, 10=highest mood). Also, write down any positive emotions you experienced before, during, or after the exercise. Try to complete one exercise a day.

Practice Date: _____

Situation: _____

_____

_____

Silver Linings:

1 _____

2. _____

3. _____

4. _____

5. _____

6. _____

Mood Before (0-10)	**Mood After (0-10)**	**Positive Emotion(s)**
_____	_____	_____

Exercise 6.1

Finding the Silver Linings

positive, neutral, or negative and find some silver linings. Let your mind go wild with this: It's good to brainstorm and come up with even silly and minor positive aspects. The goal is to let your mind find anything positive, even when the situation had a negative overtone. We want to train your brain to find the positive. Find at least six positive aspects. You may photocopy this exercise from the book or download multiple copies at the Treatments *That Work*™ website (www.oxfordclinicalpsych.com/PAT).

Try to complete one exercise per day. Identify a situation (positive, negative, neutral) and think of at least six silver linings (any positive aspect) of that situation. Record the situation above and the silver linings below, just as in the examples from Joy and Felix. Label the emotion using emotion words from Exercise 4.2: Positive Emotions Dial on page 38.

Troubleshooting for Finding the Silver Linings

I Can't Even Think of One Positive Thing!

Review the examples provided earlier. Start with an inherently positive event such as a surprise birthday party or a walk on a sunny day and try to identify silver linings in it. Remember, this is a skill to be practiced. Starting with positive events, rather than neutral or negative ones, can make it easier to get familiar with how to do this exercise. Indeed, the very fact that it is difficult for you to identify positives indicates that you are doing the right thing working on this skill!

What About Traumas? Is There a Silver Lining in Traumatic Events?

The skill of finding silver linings can be applied to stressful events (such as major natural disasters, illness, or job loss). Some events, however, are so terrible that it would not be helpful to look for silver linings, and traumas fit this description. Talking about a trauma can trigger a lot of emotional pain and is beyond this skill's scope. While finding the positive can help you recover from major stressors, applying this skill to a trauma can be too difficult and complex to navigate without professional help. For this reason, we encourage you to seek professional assistance before applying the silver linings skill to major life events that may be considered a trauma. For this exercise, we recommend that you focus on other events rather than on past traumas. That being said, some people do find incredible growth following trauma (this is known as *posttraumatic growth*). Identifying posttraumatic growth would be an example of finding a silver lining.

The next skill you will be learning is *Taking Ownership*. Taking ownership of positive events occurring in your life is just as important as noticing and appreciating that they even exist. Before positive events can be recognized, you must first believe that you can impact and influence positive things. People with anhedonia sometimes have difficulty taking credit for their role in positive

> By **taking ownership** of your contributions, you can begin to feel positive emotions such as pride, mastery, excitement, and optimism.

events. By *Taking Ownership* of your contributions, you can begin to feel the emotions such as pride, mastery, happiness, curiosity, excitement, success, respect, and optimism. This will also help you learn the connection between your actions and the positive outcome. In addition, this skill is a blueprint for how to build more positivity in your life.

Here is an example from Joy:

 Joy organized a surprise birthday party for her husband last week. She had help from other family members and hired vendors for catering and entertainment. She could have focused on all of the tasks that others did to help her; however, Joy should acknowledge her contributions to the event. Her contributions included:

- *Hiring the caterer and entertainment.*
- *Inviting her husband's friends to the party.*
- *Making sure the party was kept a secret until the moment her husband arrived.*

After this exercise, Joy's mood improved from a 4 out of 10 to a 7 out of 10.

Figure 6.3 illustrates an example of Joy's completed *Taking Ownership* exercise sheet.

Taking Ownership

Instructions: Record the date of your practice. Then identify and record a positive situation. Identify as many positive aspects (at least 6) of that situation, and write them down under Contributions. Don't forget to write down your mood before and after the exercise on a 0-10 scale (0=lowest mood, 10=highest mood). Also, write down any positive emotions you experienced before, during, or after the exercise. Try to complete one exercise a day.

Practice Date: _June 23rd, 2pm_

Situation: _My husband's surprise party_

_____

_____

Contributions:

1. _It was my idea to throw it_

2. _I organized it_

3. _I found all the vendors_

4. _I invited everyone to come_

5. _I kept it secret from my husband_

6. _I convinced my kids to help_

Mood Before (0-10)	Mood After (0-10)	Positive Emotion(s)
4	7	Affection, excitement, pride

Figure 6.3

Joy's completed *Taking Ownership* exercise.

Now it's your turn! Using Exercise 6.2: Taking Ownership, identify a positive situation from this past week and think of all the contributions that you made to that situation. After you jot down your contributions, read them aloud slowly to yourself. Then take a moment and sit with each one. What emotions do you notice? Do you feel emotions like pride, accomplishment, contentment, or optimism? And what do you notice in your body—do you

---

Taking Ownership

Instructions: Record the date of your practice. Then identify and record a positive situation. Identify as many positive aspects (at least 6) of that situation, and write them down under Contributions. Don't forget to write down your mood before and after the exercise on a 0-10 scale (0=lowest mood, 10=highest mood). Also, write down any positive emotions you experienced before, during, or after the exercise. Try to complete one exercise a day.

Practice Date: _____

Situation: _____

_____

_____

Contributions:

1. _____

2. _____

3. _____

4. _____

5. _____

6. _____

Mood Before (0-10)	**Mood After (0-10)**	**Positive Emotion(s)**
_____	_____	_____

Exercise 6.2

Taking Ownership

feel a lightness, excitement, or warmth, for example? Label the emotions using emotion words from Exercise 4.2: Positive Emotions Dial on page 38.

Try to complete one exercise each day. You may photocopy this exercise from the book or download multiple copies at the Treatments *That Work™* website (www.oxfordclinicalpsych.com/PAT).

Troubleshooting for Taking Ownership

I Don't Have Any Positive Events In My Life

If you find yourself thinking that you don't have any positive events in your life, review your positive activities or silver linings. Each positive activity you complete and each silver lining is a positive situation or event that you can use in this skill. Positive activities that lead to a sense of mastery (such as cleaning your apartment or completing a project) are great situations to use for *Taking Ownership*! That is, you are taking action toward improving your mood.

Imagining the Positive

Now you are going to work on the skill of *Imagining the Positive* by anticipating future events as being positive. Imagining that events will turn out negatively results in a negative mood, which can also lead to decreased motivation to do things and increased thoughts of hopelessness and failure. Similarly, imagining events turning out positively will improve your mood and motivation to engage in those activities and positive activities more generally.

> By **imagining positive events** happening in the future, you can train your brain to start anticipating positive events.

Let's take the example of Joy from chapter 5 on Positive Activity Scheduling. Joy's activity was to prepare dinner for her friend Sam. Imagine how Joy would have felt if she was only able to imagine the planned dinner's negative outcomes, such as the food getting burned or her friend canceling at the last minute. Correct! She would have felt defeated and anxious before even starting her planning. How would imagining mostly negative outcomes affect Joy's behavior? She would most likely have felt a decrease in her motivation and a lack of drive to follow through. Maybe she would have even canceled the dinner altogether.

How would her motivation, thoughts, and feelings be different if she purposefully focused on imagining positive outcomes? Correct! She would have most likely felt more optimistic, joyful, and energized to get the dinner organized.

Let's continue with the same example from Joy:

 Prior to preparing dinner for her friend Sam, Joy purposefully focused on imagining positive outcomes for the dinner—for instance, the meal prep was finished on time, the meal turned out well, and the weather allowed them to eat outside in her garden. (Joy would continue imagining the rest of the event in her mind or finish writing it down.) At the end of the practice, Joy noticed her mood increasing from a 5 out of 10 to an 8 out of 10. She attributed some of this increase in mood to imagining the positive as vividly as she could (9 out of 10) and noticing positive emotions of warmth, pride, and connection that arose during the practice.

Figure 6.4 is an example of Joy's *Imagining the Positive* practice.

Imagining the Positive

Instructions: Identify a possible future event. Describe the future event with the best possible outcome. Write it as if it were happening right now (present tense), using details of your emotions, thoughts, and physical sensation (e.g., sight, smell, hearing).

It's still sunny and warm at 5pm before Sam arrives. This means that we can have dinner outside on the patio with the flowers from my garden surrounding us, and I can show off my new herbs. I can feel my heart flutter a little and a smile appears on my face. I am able to finish meal prepping early, so that all that's left is to put the lasagna in the oven. It smells incredible. Although it's a little burnt, it's the way my husband and I like it with crispy cheese on top. Sam arrives fashionably late; she greets me with a warm smile, a hug, and a compliment — "Wow. That smells incredible!," followed by another compliment — "Your garden is lovely." A large smile appears on my face...

- -

Now imagine this vividly. Don't forget to write down your mood before and after the exercise on a 0-10 scale (0=lowest mood, 10=highest mood), as well as the vividness of the recounting (10=most vivid). Also, write down any positive emotions you experienced before, during, or after the exercise. Try to complete one per day.

Mood Before (0-10)	Mood After (0-10)	Vividness (0-10)	Positive Emotion(s)
5	8	9	Warmth, pride, connection

Figure 6.4

Joy's completed *Imagining the Positive* exercise.

Here is an example from Felix:

Felix imagined calling his friend Mason to invite him to meet for coffee. Felix included thoughts, feelings, and physical sensations during his imaginal practice, which resulted in more vivid imagery and a boost in mood from a 3 out 10 to a 5 out of 10.

Figure 6.5 is an example of Felix's *Imagining the Positive* practice.

Imagining the Positive

Instructions: Identify a possible future event. Describe the future event with the best possible outcome. Write it as if it were happening right now (present tense), using details of your emotions, thoughts, and physical sensation (e.g., sight, smell, hearing).

I am noticing my heart race as I go to pick up the phone and invite my friend, Mason, to coffee. However, I am able to remind myself that this is a healthy step and that Mason likes me. These positive thoughts motivate me to dial his number. Mason picks up the phone within a few rings, and says, "Hey Man! What's up? It's been a while, but so good to hear from you." I can feel all of my muscles relax, and I think, "He is glad I called." I ask him how he is doing and then explain the reason for my calling. My voice is steady, and it doesn't seem he notices any of my anxiety. Mason expresses gratitude for my invitation for coffee. He said he had been meaning to call me himself. We work through the details...

- -

Now imagine this vividly. Don't forget to write down your mood before and after the exercise on a 0-10 scale (0=lowest mood, 10=highest mood), as well as the vividness of the recounting (10=most vivid). Also, write down any positive emotions you experienced before, during, or after the exercise. Try to complete one per day.

Mood Before (0-10)	Mood After (0-10)	Vividness (0-10)	Positive Emotion(s)
3	5	6	*Relief, excitement*

Figure 6.5

Felix's completed *Imagining the Positive* exercise.

Exercise 6.3: Imagining the Positive

Now it's your turn! Using Exercise 6.3: Imagining the Positive, rate your mood before you start. Identify a situation that will happen in the next days, for example at work, at home, or with family or friends. Imagine that situation actually happening, and make sure that your imagination is generally positive. Imagine the situation in as much detail as possible

Gently get yourself into a comfortable position with your feet flat on the ground, your back upright but not too stiff, and hands in your lap. If you feel comfortable, gently close your eyes or rest them on a spot in front of you. Bring to mind an image of your surroundings at your starting point.

Imagine where you are as vividly as possible. Notice what you see around you…smells…sounds…temperature. Do you notice a nice aroma? Do you notice sounds of nature or other noises? Is it warm or cool? Do you feel a nice breeze? Take a moment to notice your surroundings. (Pause)

Now shift your attention to your own body in that future moment. What are the physical symptoms you are feeling? Are you feeling a rush of adrenaline? A release of tension? Perhaps a positive racing of the heart or a smile on your face? (Pause)

What are the emotions you are feeling? Excitement? Peace? Joy? Curiosity? Compassion? Interest? Imagine feeling one of these positive feelings and what it might feel like in your body. (Pause)

Now identify your thoughts in this future context. How can you make them more positive? (Pause)

Begin to slowly walk yourself through the events that you wrote down on your exercise form. Take time to notice your positive thoughts, emotions, and bodily sensations as you walk yourself through those positive events. (Pause)

Notice what your future self would be feeling now . . . thinking now . . . (Allow minutes to pass)

Whenever you are ready, gently bring your attention back to the room, and open your eyes.

and as if it is playing out in real time. You can use the visualization script we provide in Box 6.1, or access the ◉ recording, which is available at this link www.oxfordclinicalpsych.com/LGTBQ_CBT. Walk yourself through the event step by step focusing on positive aspects of the situation: sights, sounds, sensations, feelings, and emotions. That means seeing the situation unfold from your own perspective—as if it is happening in front of you (rather than you observing from a distance). Include details of what you see, hear, feel, and even what you smell or taste. The details will make the imagery as powerful as possible. Try to complete one exercise each day. Label the emotion using the emotion words from Exercise 4.2: Positive Emotions Dial on page 38. You may photocopy this exercise from the book or download multiple copies at the Treatments *That Work*™ website (www.oxfordclinicalpsych.com/PAT).

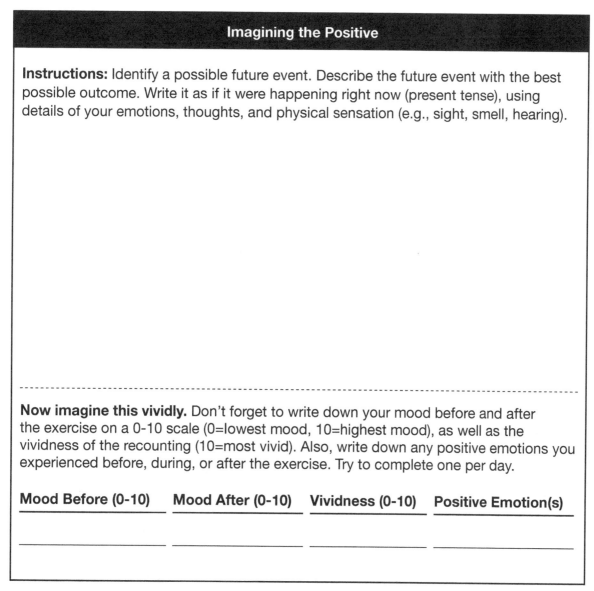

Imagining the Positive

Instructions: Identify a possible future event. Describe the future event with the best possible outcome. Write it as if it were happening right now (present tense), using details of your emotions, thoughts, and physical sensation (e.g., sight, smell, hearing).

- -

Now imagine this vividly. Don't forget to write down your mood before and after the exercise on a 0-10 scale (0=lowest mood, 10=highest mood), as well as the vividness of the recounting (10=most vivid). Also, write down any positive emotions you experienced before, during, or after the exercise. Try to complete one per day.

Mood Before (0-10)	Mood After (0-10)	Vividness (0-10)	Positive Emotion(s)

Exercise 6.3

Imagining the Positive

After doing each exercise, think about how you feel as you imagined that scene as if it were actually happening. Notice if your mood improved after the imagining. See the connection between imagining a positive outcome and how positive you feel in the moment. You may even notice your heart rate accelerates a little. You may also notice a nagging feeling that this imaginal practice is not real and that the outcome you are imagining will never really happen. Remember, the goal here is not to guarantee an outcome—we are not trying to make positive events actually happen. Instead, we are building the muscle of being able to anticipate positive events, so you can actually imagine whatever positive outcome you like—from having a nice day at the beach to becoming a world leader. However, it may work better for you to imagine things that have a real possibility of coming true.

Another nagging feeling may be that you don't deserve positive outcomes. Again, the goal here is to build the muscle of positivity through imagination.

Lastly, by imaging positive events or positive aspects within those events—whether positive, neutral, or negative—you are training your brain to pay attention to those positive aspects in the future. Using the example of a walk in the park, if we train ourselves to vividly imagine the smell of the leaves, the sound of the earth underfoot, and the laughter of children, it will make it more likely that we will attend to those positive aspects when we are actually taking a walk. It will also make it more likely that we are actually motivated to do it because now we can anticipate the positive event instead of a negative one.

Troubleshooting for Imagining the Positive

I'm Having a Difficult Time Finding an Event to Imagine

If you are having difficulty thinking of a positive event, review the items from the Positive Activity lists and see if you can imagine another one of those.

I Don't Believe That Thinking More Positively Is the Solution to My Problem

You're right: Thinking more positively is *not* the solution to your problem. But it is one part of a set of skills that will help you learn to appreciate and experience positive events more deeply. You are developing skills that will hopefully become more automatic for you and increase your mood in the long run.

Combining Attending to the Positive with Actions Toward Feeling Better

The "Attending to the Positive" skills will help you think more positively about past, future, and current events. They will allow you to better notice, feel, and appreciate the positive and foster your learning. That is, it will become easier to make connections between your efforts and a positive outcome. This is best practiced when combined with the positive actions you learned in chapter 5. Incorporating positive activities with an exercise in *Taking Ownership* is a great way to savor your role and input. *Imagining the Positive* will make it easier to identify a pleasant activity that you want to try and to improve your motivation to follow through with your plans. Likewise, *Finding the Silver Linings* is a particularly helpful exercise when you feel that an activity seemed less rewarding than you had hoped. After identifying the silver linings, you may find that the activity is worth trying again! Combining thinking skills with taking action is a fantastic way to improve your ability to savor the moment, feel motivated, and improve your memory of the events.

CHAPTER 7 ▶ Building Positivity

The Function of Building Positivity

Four practices that people have been engaging in for centuries are *Loving-Kindness*, *Appreciative Joy*, *Gratitude*, and *Generosity*. Two of these practices—*Gratitude* and *Generosity*—are universal human experiences. Science has repeatedly shown that they increase positive emotions and well-being and decrease negative emotions. There is also a lot of evidence to show that engaging in them leads to feeling more connected, having better relationships, and doing more "prosocial" behavior—behavior that benefits others.

Gratitude

Although *Gratitude* is an emotion, it is also a behavior and thinking skill. *Gratitude* is the act of noticing and appreciating the positive in this world. Some scientists have defined *Gratitude* to include:

- Appreciation of other people
- A focus on one's possessions
- Admiration for beauty
- A behavior
- Mindful awareness of the positive
- Appreciation that one's life is time-limited
- A healthy comparison to those less fortunate

Generosity

Generosity is a behavior. Science has shown that people who report more *Generosity* also report higher levels of happiness. In fact, in one research study, giving away money led to greater happiness than receiving money. However, *Generosity* is not limited to material goods. It can be giving one's time (for example, instead of paying for a friend's cab, driving them home). People who volunteer have improved health, live a longer life, and are less depressed. In fact, research shows that one person's act of *Generosity* increases the likelihood that someone else will do a generous act! This means that generosity is a wonderful way to boost one's positive mood.

Loving-Kindness and Appreciative Joy

Unlike *Generosity* and *Gratitude*, *Loving-Kindness* and *Appreciative Joy* are less known outside of Eastern spiritual practices. They have their origins from the Buddhist tradition and have been shown to improve positive mood, decrease negative mood, and enhance feelings of connectedness toward others. *Loving-Kindness* is a practice that enhances feelings of love and kindness by offering positive thoughts toward others, oneself, and the world. *Appreciative Joy* is a practice that generates positive emotions emerging from the success of others.

In sum, "Building Positivity" exercises are strategies to enhance your mood. *Loving-Kindness* and *Appreciative Joy* are two skills that use imagery and positive thinking to improve relationships and change how you feel. *Gratitude* and *Generosity* are behavioral and thinking skills that have been shown to improve mood. The goal of all four skills is to enhance your ability to notice and appreciate the positive (liking) and to learn to form connections between the act of giving or receiving and positive mood (learning).

Practicing Loving-Kindness

Loving-Kindness is a practice that will help you increase positive emotions, like love, kindness, warmth, compassion, connectedness, joy, and openness. You will visualize sending out positive thoughts that will help build a deep connection to others, the world, and yourself.

> **Loving-Kindness** is a practice that enhances feelings of love and kindness by offering positive thoughts toward others, oneself, and the world.

Here is an example from Joy:

 Joy practiced Loving-Kindness first with her dog as the recipient, then a close friend, and finally herself. Joy noted that the exercise became harder as she transitioned from her pet to her friend and from her friend to herself. She noticed that she began to feel as though she wasn't genuine. Despite these thoughts, Joy continued to practice the skill, and the negative thoughts went away over time. She noticed that she began to feel more peaceful both in her mind and body. She also reported feeling love and amusement. Her mood improved from a 5 out of 10 to a 6 out of 10.

Figure 7.1 shows an example of Joy's completed *Loving-Kindness* exercise sheet.

Loving-Kindness

Instructions: Record the date of your practice. Identify at least one recipient of your *Loving-Kindness* practice. It can be helpful to start with someone uncomplicated. Read or listen to the *Loving-Kindness* script or recording. Be sure to record your mood (0=lowest, 10=highest) before and after your practice, as well as any positive emotions, thoughts, or physical sensations you notice. Try to complete one per day.

Practice Date: _____ June 6 _____

Recipient(s) of Practice: ___ My dog, close friend ___

Mood Before (0-10): ___ 3 _____

Mood After (0-10): ___ 7 _____

Positive Emotion(s): ___ love, peaceful, amused ___

_____

Reaction (thoughts, physical sensations):

Smile, warmth in chest, some muscle tension,

"I have the cutest puppy ever,"

"This feels a little silly and odd,"

"This feels a little disingenuous"

Figure 7.1

Joy's completed *Loving-Kindness* exercise.

Here is an example from Felix:

 Felix practiced Loving-Kindness first with his mom as recipient, then a friend, and then himself. Felix noticed that he enjoyed the exercise and immediately began to feel calm, relaxed, loved, and cared about. His mood improved from a 4 out of 10 to a 7 out of 10.

Figure 7.2 shows an example of Felix's completed *Loving-Kindness* exercise sheet.

Loving-Kindness

Instructions: Record the date of your practice. Identify at least one recipient of your *Loving-Kindness* practice. It can be helpful to start with someone uncomplicated. Read or listen to the *Loving-Kindness* script or recording. Be sure to record your mood (0=lowest, 10=highest) before and after your practice, as well as any positive emotions, thoughts, or physical sensations you notice. Try to complete one per day.

Practice Date: _November 7_

Recipient(s) of Practice: _Mom, friend, me_

Mood Before (0-10): _4_

Mood After (0-10): _7_

Positive Emotion(s): _Calm, loved, cared about_

Reaction (thoughts, physical sensations):

"My mom really loves me," release of physical tension, "I feel cared about," "I think this exercise actually works"

Figure 7.2

Felix's completed *Loving-Kindness* exercise.

Exercise 7.1: Loving-Kindness

Now it's your turn! The instructions in Box 7.1 will guide you through this skill, although this practice works best when you listen to the 🔊 audio recording, which is available at this link www.oxfordclinicalpsych.com/ LGTBQ_CBT. However, if you choose not to use the audio recording to practice the skill, read the guided instructions before practicing the exercise.

Box 7.1 Guided Instructions for Practicing Loving-Kindness

Find a comfortable position someplace with little to no distractions. It can be helpful to sit in a chair with your feet flat on the ground, your back upright, and your eyes closed or gently resting on a spot in front of you.

If you notice that your mind is racing, wandering, or being especially distractible today, take a moment to gently shift your attention to your breath, by noticing each inhalation and each exhalation. Observe the changes in your body as you take air in and as you release it. Notice your belly rising and falling or the change in temperature of the air traveling in and out of your nose.

Whenever you are ready, begin by identifying someone who you like and who is uncomplicated. This can be someone who you deeply care about, even a pet, or it can be someone who you know from a distance but greatly respect . . . Imagine them sitting in front of you, smiling, and looking back at you.

Offer them the following statements, focusing on the words as you say them aloud or in your mind.

> *I wish you peace . . .*
>
> *I wish you health . . .*
>
> *I hope you are without distress, hardship, and misfortune . . .*
>
> *I wish you love and joy . . .*
>
> *. . .*
>
> *I wish you peace . . .*
>
> *I wish you health . . .*
>
> *I hope you are without distress, hardship, and misfortune . . .*
>
> *I wish you love and joy . . .*

Notice what emotions and physical sensations emerge as you offer these statements. Warmth? A smile? It's also okay to not notice any positive emotions right now.

> *I wish you peace . . .*
>
> *I wish you health . . .*
>
> *I hope you are without distress, hardship, and misfortune . . .*
>
> *I wish you love and joy . . .*

(continued)

Box 7.1 Continued

Take a moment now to shift back to your breath, noticing the rise and fall of your belly with each inhalation and exhalation.

Now bring to mind someone who is a little more difficult. It can be a difficult family member, work colleague, or political figure. It can even be yourself. It should not be anyone who has abused you or was the cause of a trauma. Once you have chosen this individual, imagine them sitting in front of you. Offer them the following statements:

> *I wish to feel at peace or I wish you peace . . .*
>
> *I wish for good health or I wish you health . . .*
>
> *I hope that I am or you are without distress, hardship, and misfortune . . .*
>
> *I wish that I or you experience love and joy . . .*
>
> *. . .*
>
> *I wish to feel at peace or I wish you peace . . .*
>
> *I wish for good health or I wish you health . . .*
>
> *I hope that I am or you are without distress, hardship, and misfortune . . .*
>
> *I wish that I or you experience love and joy . . .*

Notice any emotions or physical feelings that arise.

> *I wish to feel at peace or I wish you peace . . .*
>
> *I wish for good health or I wish you health . . .*
>
> *I hope that I am or you are without distress, hardship, and misfortune . . .*
>
> *I wish that I or you experience love and joy . . .*

Return again to your breath for the next few moments, take a few deep breaths if you notice yourself being especially distractible.

Now bring to mind an image of the world, offering positive thoughts.

> *I wish the world peace . . .*
>
> *I wish the world health . . .*
>
> *I hope the world is without distress, hardship, and misfortune . . .*

(continued)

I wish the world love and joy . . .

. . .

I wish the world peace . . .

I wish the world health . . .

I hope the world is without distress, hardship, and misfortune . . .

I wish the world love and joy . . .

Now what emotions and physical symptoms arise?

For the final time, gently shift your attention to your breath . . . and then open your eyes.

Using an Exercise 7.1: Loving-Kindness sheet, first choose someone simple—an uncomplicated person, such as a friend or mentor, or a pet, and then move on to more difficult people. That is, we start by thinking about someone who easily brings on *loving and kind* thoughts. It may even be a loved one who has passed. For many people, this practice can be difficult, and if that is the case for you, that's okay. Like all of the skills that you have learned in this treatment, the more you practice, the easier it will become, and the greater benefit you will receive from it. Therefore, if you notice frustration or other negative emotions during your practice, that's okay and can be expected early on.

Complete at least one practice per day (ideally no less than three times during the next week). You may photocopy this exercise from the book or download multiple copies at the Treatments *That Work*™ website (www.oxfordclinicalpsych.com/PAT). Before starting, make sure to record your mood and write down the recipient you are sending love and kindness to. Also record your mood after completing the exercise, along with any other thoughts, feelings, and physical sensations you noticed.

Loving-Kindness

Instructions: Record the date of your practice. Identify at least one recipient of your *Loving-Kindness* practice. It can be helpful to start with someone uncomplicated. Read or listen to the *Loving-Kindness* script or recording. Be sure to record your mood (0=lowest mood, 10=highest mood) before and after your practice, as well as any positive emotions, thoughts, or physical sensations you notice. Try to complete one per day.

Practice Date: _____

Recipient(s) of Practice: _____

Mood Before (0-10): _____

Mood After (0-10): _____

Positive Emotion(s): _____

_____

Reaction (thoughts, physical sensations):

_____

_____

_____

_____

Exercise 7.1

Loving-Kindness

Troubleshooting for Practicing Loving-Kindness

I Only Feel More Depressed, Anxious, Jealous, or Angry When I Practice Loving-Kindness. Is Something Wrong with Me?

It is not surprising that a lot of these feelings are arising. There is nothing wrong with you. It is quite natural to have these emotions arise. For many people, this skill is really difficult. Try to stick with the practice and see what happens to these emotions and whether new emotions arise. If you decide that this is not a skill you will continue on your own, that's fine. It may also mean that you are practicing with someone who is too difficult to practice *Loving-Kindness* with in that moment. You can always try returning to someone who is less complicated, such as a pet. Notice what feelings arise for them, and then you can later return to a more complicated person.

I'm Not Feeling Positive Emotions. Am I Doing Something Wrong?

You are not doing anything wrong. For a lot of people, this practice is really difficult at first. Try to give it time and practice and see what happens to your emotions and whether new emotions arise. If you decide that this is not a practice you will continue on your own, that's fine.

Is Loving-Kindness the Same as Praying?

Loving-Kindness is the practice of mentally offering positive statements to another being. In some forms of prayer, the individual praying can decide to ask a higher power to provide for another being. Although both prayer and *Loving-Kindness* can look similar on the surface, there are differences. While prayer can take many forms, *Loving-Kindness* is a specific practice of offering statements regarding general health, well-being, and happiness. Also, unlike *Loving-Kindness*, prayer requires that there is a higher power for one to pray to. A benefit of *Loving-Kindness* is that both people of a spiritual faith and of non-religious background can practice it and still find benefit.

It Feels Awkward, Not Genuine, Too Fluffy, and "Mushy Gushy"

A lot of people feel this way, especially when first beginning to practice *Loving-Kindness*. If you notice this happening for you, continue with the skill anyway and see if the awkwardness or disingenuity gets better.

I Can't Even Think of Someone Who Is Uncomplicated!

For some people, this part is the most difficult. If no one seems uncomplicated, think of a person or pet who brings the least amount of negative emotion, including individuals in your past.

Gratitude is an emotion, behavior, and thinking skill. It involves noticing and appreciating the positive that surrounds us and learning to form connections between the act of being grateful and positive mood. There are many benefits to practicing *Gratitude*. Science has shown that *Gratitude*:

> **Gratitude** involves *Identifying the Silver Linings* in your day, week, or life that you appreciate.

- Enhances well-being
- Increases positive emotions
- Decreases negative emotions and stress
- Improves health and connection with others
- Increases generosity

There are many different ways to practice *Gratitude*, and you will practice one method in this treatment. Using Exercise 7.2: Gratitude (see page 98), you will list five things to be grateful for each day, and each item must be different from what you listed the previous day. This may seem like an impossible task at first. Remember though that you are now an expert in *Finding the Silver Linings*, which will help with this new skill. *Gratitude* means identifying the silver linings or positive aspects in your day, week, or life that you appreciate. It is important to keep in mind that we can be grateful for any number of things, as simple as taking a single breath at a given moment or as complicated as being in therapy! Remember, *Finding the Silver Linings* and *Gratitude* items can be major (e.g., "I am grateful for having my son in my life"), minor (e.g., "I am thankful for making it to work on time"), and even silly (e.g., "I am grateful for my soap, which keeps me from being smelly!").

At the end of the week, you will have a list of 35 things to be thankful for. You can add and return to this list as needed throughout the rest of treatment and beyond, especially on days when everything might seem to be going poorly. This list can be a helpful reminder of the positive that is present.

Making *Gratitude* a behavior that you practice daily as part of your routine will help you get the most out of this skill. Therefore, we encourage you to pick a regular time to complete this list each day and set a reminder on your phone. Most people prefer to complete this exercise in the evening and to reflect back on their day.

Here is an example from Felix:

Felix completed his Gratitude list before going to bed to reflect on the day. On the first day, his list included seeing wildlife on his morning walk, texting with a friend, cuddling up with his cat, having the ingredients he needed to make macaroni and cheese, and going to bed on time. His mood improved from a 4 out of 10 to an 8 out of 10.

Figure 7.3 shows an example of Felix's completed *Gratitude* exercise sheet.

Gratitude

Instructions: Record the date of your practice. List 5 things you notice and appreciate each day, making sure that they are different from the previous day. Record your mood (0=lowest mood, 10=highest mood) before and after making the list. Also, write down any positive emotions you notice. Try to complete one exercise per day.

Date: September 15

Today I am grateful for...

1. Seeing wildlife on morning walk
2. Texting with Johnny
3. My cat cuddling with me
4. Having the ingredients to make mac–n–cheese
5. Going to bed on time

Mood Before (0-10): 4

Mood After (0-10): 8

Positive Emotion(s): Grateful, joy

Figure 7.3

Felix's completed *Gratitude* list.

Here is an example from Joy:

 Joy decided to complete her Gratitude list while getting ready for bed. On the first day, her list included waking up on time, drinking coffee from her favorite mug, having lunch with a colleague, speaking with her daughter on the phone, and watching TV with her husband. Her mood improved from a 6 out of 10 to a 9 out of 10.

Figure 7.4 shows an example of Joy's completed *Gratitude* exercise sheet.

Gratitude

Instructions: Record the date of your practice. List 5 things you notice and appreciate each day, making sure that they are different from the previous day. Record your mood (0=lowest mood, 10=highest mood) before and after making the list. Also, write down any positive emotions you notice. Try to complete one exercise per day.

Date: _March 22_

Today I am grateful for...

1. _Waking up on time_
2. _Drinking coffee from my favorite mug_
3. _Lunch with colleague_
4. _Speaking with my daughter on the phone_
5. _Watching my favorite show with my husband_

Mood Before (0-10): _6_

Mood After (0-10): _9_

Positive Emotion(s): _Content, hopeful_

Figure 7.4

Joy's completed *Gratitude* list.

Exercise 7.2: Gratitude

Now it's your turn! Using Exercise 7.2: Gratitude, list five things you notice and appreciate each day, making sure they are different from the previous day. Record your mood before and after completing the practice. Complete at least one practice per day (no less than three times during the next week). You may photocopy this exercise from the book or download multiple copies at the Treatments *That Work*™ website (www.oxfordclinicalpsych.com/PAT).

Gratitude

Instructions: Record the date of your practice. List 5 things you notice and appreciate each day, making sure that they are different from the previous day. Record your mood (0=lowest mood, 10=highest mood) before and after making the list. Also, write down any positive emotions you notice. Try to complete one exercise per day.

Date: _____

Today I am grateful for...

1. _____

2. _____

3. _____

4. _____

5. _____

Mood Before (0-10): _____

Mood After (0-10): _____

Positive Emotion(s): _____

_____

Exercise 7.2

Gratitude

Troubleshooting for Practicing Gratitude

I Can't Think of Anything I'm Grateful For

This is a common response and one reason you are seeking out this treatment! Returning to your work with *Finding the Silver Linings* can help. Try completing one to three silver linings for today, and notice how those items are also things to be grateful for!

I Can't Think of Five Things to Be Grateful For

Try to be creative. If not, focusing on one or two things is okay.

Generosity is the act of giving by choice and without expecting something in return. Being generous can be challenging for many reasons. We all have limited time and resources, and we might fear not having enough to give. This fear might be based on truth for some of us if we think about *Generosity* very narrowly. For example, if we believe that *Generosity* is only about giving away money or volunteering time, we might not actually have enough resources to be generous regularly. However, *Generosity* can be unlimited if we recognize the many forms it can take, including time, energy, money, physical help, advice, knowledge/information, compassion, and love. Being generous can look like a smile, kind words, or a listening ear. It could be helping a friend, an animal, nature, a cause, or yourself. The options you have for being generous are endless. *Generosity* will help with:

- Noticing and appreciating the positive
- Enhancing positive emotions
- Learning to form connections between the act of giving and the feeling of positive emotions

Surprisingly, research has shown that being generous improves our mood more than receiving something. *Generosity* is associated with:

- Health
- Decreased negative emotions and stress
- Improved relationships

Also, being generous increases the likelihood of getting something in return!

> **Generosity** is the act of giving by choice and without expecting something in return.

Here is an example from Joy:

Joy scheduled three acts of Generosity into her week, including driving her son to the airport, helping her husband with yardwork, and donating $50 to a local charity. She noticed that driving her son to the airport made her feel cheerful and valued; her mood improved from a 5 out of 10 to an 8 out of 10.

Figure 7.5 shows an example of Joy's completed *Generosity* exercise sheet.

Generosity

Instructions: Record the date and time of your generous act. Identify and record what your generous act will be and who will be the recipient of it. Record your mood (0=lowest mood, 10=highest mood) before and after doing the generous act. Also write down any positive emotions you notice. Try to complete 3 per week.

Date/Time: _July 28, 4pm_

Act: _Drive son to airport_

Recipient: _Son_

Mood Before (0-10): _5_

Mood After (0-10): _8_

Positive Emotion(s): _Cheerful, valued_

Figure 7.5

Joy's completed *Generosity* exercise.

Here is an example from Felix:

Felix decided that he would help his elderly neighbor take out the trash, assist his mom with groceries, and order a present for a friend online. After helping his neighbor take out the trash, Felix noted that he felt productive and proud. He recorded that his mood improved from a 3 out of 10 to a 6 out of 10.

Figure 7.6 shows an example of Felix's completed *Generosity* exercise sheet.

Generosity

Instructions: Record the date and time of your generous act. Identify and record what your generous act will be and who will be the recipient of it. Record your mood (0=lowest mood, 10=highest mood) before and after doing the generous act. Also write down any positive emotions you notice. Try to complete 3 per week.

Date/Time : *Saturday morning*

Act: *Help neighbor take out trash*

Recipient: *Neighbor*

Mood Before (0-10): *3*

Mood After (0-10): *6*

Positive Emotion(s): *productive, proud*

Figure 7.6

Felix's completed *Generosity* exercise.

Exercise 7.3: Generosity

Now it's your turn! Using Exercise 7.3: Generosity, identify three acts of generosity to practice this week. Schedule them into your week by writing down the day and time you plan to do them. You will use one form/sheet per generous act. Record your mood before and after doing each exercise. You may photocopy this exercise from the book or download multiple copies at the Treatments *That Work*™ website (www.oxfordclinicalpsych.com/PAT). Once you have completed these acts of *Generosity*, it can be especially helpful to practice savoring these activities.

Generosity

Instructions: Record the date and time of your generous act. Identify and record what your generous act will be and who will be the recipient of it. Record your mood (0= lowest mood, 10=highest mood) before and after doing the generous act. Also, write down any positive emotions you notice. Try to complete 3 per week.

Date/Time: _____

Act: _____

Recipient: _____

Mood Before (0-10): _____

Mood After (0-10): _____

Positive Emotion(s): _____

_____

Exercise 7.3

Generosity

Troubleshooting for Practicing Generosity

If I Give, There Won't Be Enough for Me

Often we do not engage in generous acts because we are afraid of not having enough. What we learn when practicing *Generosity* is that *Generosity* can take many forms. *Generosity* can be free of cost, time, and energy, like offering a smile to someone or thinking a positive thought about them. However, you may discover that the most generous act is recognizing your own needs (e.g., self-care) and giving yourself the space to attend to those needs. When you notice having the thought, "There won't be enough for me," observe what is going on in your mind and body. Reflect on the following: What is the motivation behind this act of *Generosity*? Is it motivated by duty or desire to be appreciated? Is this really an act of *Generosity* or something to make yourself feel better? Is the other person really benefiting from this act? Then ask yourself, "What is the most generous act in this moment?"

What's the Point If I Am Not or My Behavior Is Not Appreciated?

Remember that our goal here in therapy is to generate positive emotions and engage in the act of *Generosity*, even if that means *not* receiving something in return. Giving with the belief that you should get something in return often leads to regret instead of positive emotions. You have the choice of giving with or without regret.

I Already Engage in a Lot of Generosity

That's great! Some people tend to be more or less generous in their daily lives. If you already give too much to others, try being generous to yourself. Examples of being generous to yourself include giving yourself a mini-vacation, treating yourself to a massage, taking a bath, choosing to spend time with friends at work, or giving yourself a break for not being perfect.

I Am Worried About How People Will Respond

The positive mood generated from *Generosity* does not stem from another's demonstration of their appreciation. Instead, the positive mood emerges from the actual act of giving. Therefore, when we focus on the outcome rather than the process, we are losing the positive benefits of those generous acts. *Generosity* requires letting go of the outcome.

Appreciative Joy is the feeling of joy or other positive emotions in response to someone else's joy or fortune. It is also a practice similar to *Loving-Kindness*. You will use imagery and visualization to offer fortune and success to others and notice the emotions that arise when doing so. This is a skill that can bring up feelings of admiration, pride, joy, love, and connection, and it is the opposite of finding joy from the misfortune of others. Like *Loving-Kindness*, *Appreciative Joy* can generate a feeling of connection to others.

> **Appreciative Joy** is the experience of positive emotions that emerge from the success of others.

Here is an example from Felix:

 Felix had difficulty engaging in this exercise. He finds it hard to offer others success when he struggles with his own. He started the exercise by thinking about a close friend and wishing him good things and happiness. He noticed that he feels happy for his friend but also that his mood improved (from a 3 out of 10 to a 4 out of 10). Over time, Felix began to notice feelings of closeness, connection, and warmth, and realized that his mood improved with each practice.

Figure 7.7 shows an example of Felix's completed *Appreciative Joy* exercise sheet.

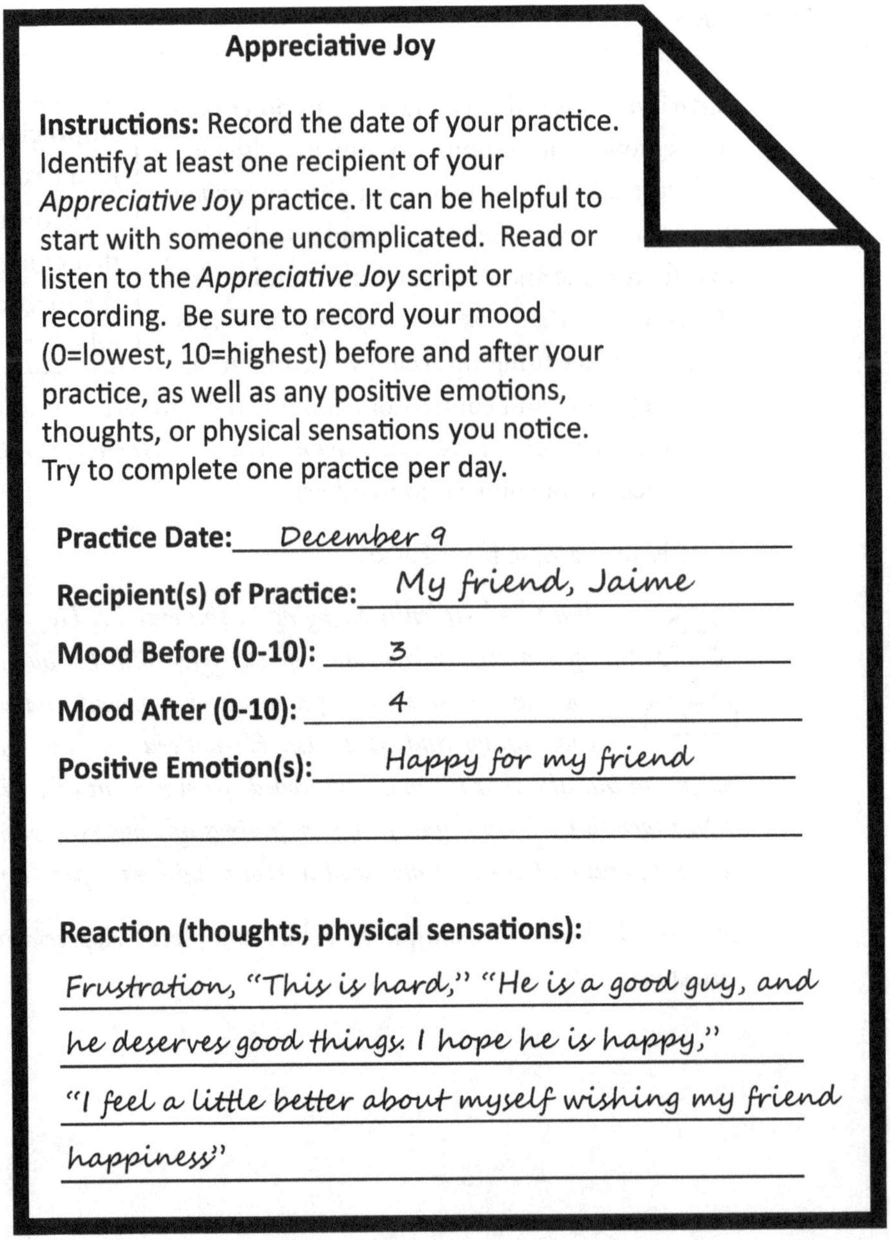

Appreciative Joy

Instructions: Record the date of your practice. Identify at least one recipient of your *Appreciative Joy* practice. It can be helpful to start with someone uncomplicated. Read or listen to the *Appreciative Joy* script or recording. Be sure to record your mood (0=lowest, 10=highest) before and after your practice, as well as any positive emotions, thoughts, or physical sensations you notice. Try to complete one practice per day.

Practice Date: _December 9_

Recipient(s) of Practice: _My friend, Jaime_

Mood Before (0-10): _3_

Mood After (0-10): _4_

Positive Emotion(s): _Happy for my friend_

Reaction (thoughts, physical sensations):
Frustration, "This is hard," "He is a good guy, and
he deserves good things. I hope he is happy,"
"I feel a little better about myself wishing my friend
happiness"

Figure 7.7

Felix's completed *Appreciative Joy* exercise.

Here is an example from Joy:

 Joy practiced Appreciative Joy by wishing good fortune and success to her husband. She noticed experiencing comfort and joy. She also felt warmth, satisfaction, and love. Her mood improved from a 4 out of 10 to a 7 out of 10.

Figure 7.8 shows an example of Joy's completed *Appreciative Joy* exercise sheet.

Appreciative Joy

Instructions: Record the date of your practice. Identify at least one recipient of your *Appreciative Joy* practice. It can be helpful to start with someone uncomplicated. Read or listen to the *Appreciative Joy* script or recording. Be sure to record your mood (0=lowest, 10=highest) before and after your practice, as well as any positive emotions, thoughts, or physical sensations you notice. Try to complete one practice per day.

Practice Date: July 29

Recipient(s) of Practice: My husband

Mood Before (0-10): 4

Mood After (0-10): 7

Positive Emotion(s): Love, satisfaction, comfort

Reaction (thoughts, physical sensations):

Warmth, smile, "I love my husband so much, and am so happy he is doing well," "I want to share with my husband how I feel"

Figure 7.8

Joy's completed *Appreciative Joy* exercise.

Exercise 7.4: Appreciative Joy

Now it's your turn! The instructions in Box 7.2 will guide you through this skill, although this practice works best when you listen to the 🔊 audio recording, which is available at this link: www.oxfordclinicalpsych. com/LGTBQ_CBT

Box 7.2 Guided Instructions for Practicing Appreciative Joy

Find a comfortable position someplace with little to no distractions. It can be helpful to sit in a chair with your feet flat on the ground, your back upright, and your eyes closed or gently resting on a spot in front of you.

If you notice that your mind is racing, wandering, or being especially distractible today, take a moment to gently shift your attention to your breath, by noticing each inhalation and each exhalation. Observe the changes in your body as you take air in and as you release it. Notice your belly rising and falling or the change in temperature of the air traveling in and out of your nose.

Whenever you are ready, begin by identifying someone who you like and who is uncomplicated. This can be someone who you deeply care about, even a pet, or it can be someone who you know from a distance but greatly respect . . . Imagine them sitting in front of you, smiling, and looking back at you.

Identify one good fortune that they have. Notice the emotions that arise as you identify what that is.

Offer them the following statements, focusing on the words as you say them aloud or in your mind.

I am happy you are happy and content . . .

I hope your success stays with you . . .

I hope your wealth continues to grow . . .

. . .

I am happy you are happy and content . . .

I hope your success stays with you . . .

I hope your wealth continues to grow . . .

Notice what emotions and physical sensations emerge as you offer these statements. Joy? A smile? It's also okay to not have any positive emotions right now.

(continued)

Box 7.2 Continued

Take a moment to shift your attention back to your breath, noticing the rise and fall of your belly with each inhalation and exhalation.

Now bring to mind someone who is a little more difficult. It can be yourself, a friend, or a family member. Once you have chosen this individual, imagine them sitting in front of you.

Identify one good fortune that they have. Notice the emotions that arise as you identify what that is. Offer them the following statements:

I am happy you are happy and content . . .

I hope your success stays with you . . .

I hope your wealth continues to grow . . .

. . .

I am happy you are happy and content . . .

I hope your success stays with you . . .

I hope your wealth continues to grow . . .

Notice any emotions or physical feelings that arise.

For the final time, gently shift your attention to your breath . . . and then open your eyes.

Using Exercise 7.4: Appreciative Joy, complete at least one practice per day (no less than three times in the next week). Record your mood before and after doing each exercise along with any other thoughts, feelings, and physical sensations you noticed. You may photocopy this exercise from the book or download multiple copies at the Treatments *That Work*™ website (www.oxfordclinicalpsych.com/PAT).

Appreciative Joy

Instructions: Record the date of your practice. Identify at least one recipient of your *Appreciative Joy* practice. It can be helpful to start with someone uncomplicated. Read or listen to the *Appreciative Joy* script or recording. Be sure to record your mood (0=lowest mood, 10=highest mood) before and after your practice, as well as any positive emotions, thoughts, or physical sensations you notice. Try to complete one practice per day.

Practice Date: _____

Recipient(s) of Practice: _____

Mood Before (0-10): _____

Mood After (0-10): _____

Positive Emotion(s): _____

Reaction (thoughts, physical sensations):

_____

_____

_____

_____

_____

Exercise 7.4

Appreciative Joy

Troubleshooting for Practicing Appreciative Joy

I Feel Jealous: I Can't Feel Any Appreciative Joy

Sometimes we feel jealousy instead of joy for others. Validate what you are feeling by telling yourself, "I am human, and sometimes I feel this way," while also recognizing that these emotions may change with more practice. When you are ready, we recommend trying again. It often takes time before feeling positive emotions with *Appreciative Joy*.

Is Appreciative Joy the Same as Praying?

Appreciative Joy is the joy one feels from another being's success or fortune and is the practice of mentally offering positive statements to another being. Although *Appreciative Joy* practices and praying have similarities, they are not the same. While prayer can take many forms, *Appreciative Joy* is a specific skill of offering statements of happiness for another being's fortune. Also, unlike *Appreciative Joy*, prayer requires a higher power to whom one prays. A benefit of *Appreciative Joy* is that both people of a spiritual faith and of non-religious background can practice it and still find benefit.

Putting It All Together: Building Positivity, Engaging in Positive Activities, and Attending to the Positive

Because the "Building Positivity" exercises in this chapter are a combination of thought and behavioral strategies, they are best practiced when combined with the skills you learned in earlier chapters. Incorporating *Generosity* as a positive activity into your week for *Savoring the Moment* is a wonderful way to get the most out of these skills. *Gratitude* and *Finding the Silver Linings* are closely linked, and using *Finding the Silver Linings* to help you identify things to be grateful for can be beneficial. Also, *Loving-Kindness* and *Appreciative Joy* can be fantastic motivators for engaging in social activities as part of your behavioral exercises. Similar to *Imagining the Positive*, they use imagery. In this treatment, we suggest that you practice each new skill first before combining them.

You might find that some of these skills are easier to learn than others. For example, if you struggle with imagery or visualization, you may not enjoy *Loving-Kindness* and *Appreciative Joy*. That's okay. We encourage you to practice each skill for at least one week daily, and if you are still struggling to find some benefit, you can move on to the next skill. If you are struggling to identify *Gratitude* items, we encourage you to return to *Finding the Silver Linings*, which will help you identify things to be thankful for. Finally, if you find yourself overwhelmed by the skill of *Generosity* because you already devote so much of your resources to others, then we encourage you to practice this skill on yourself. Acts of *Generosity* to oneself can include taking a mini-vacation, going for a walk, taking a bath, cooking a favorite meal, visiting the doctor, and buying a special gift for yourself.

Treatment Gains and Relapse Prevention

CHAPTER 8

Continuing the Journey After Treatment

Progress Assessment

Congratulations! You have completed all the core components of the Positive Affect Treatment (PAT)! One of the fundamental goals of this therapy was to help you notice and appreciate the positive. Therefore, it is important to pause, notice, and appreciate the steps that you have taken. They are significant accomplishments that are worth taking ownership of and giving yourself some much-deserved praise for. See if you can identify any emotions that you are feeling right now. Perhaps pride? Maybe excitement? Once you have allowed yourself to savor the accomplishments you made in treatment, it can be helpful to review the progress you have made to determine the next steps. While learning the skills offered in this treatment is a success in and of itself, it is important that you assess the kind of progress you have made to guide your decisions around whether you need to return to some skills for additional work. Some people learn that certain skills need additional weeks of daily practice after completing the progress assessment (see Exercise 8.1) before fully moving on to treatment completion.

It is important to mention that not everyone feels good about finishing treatment because it can be scary to think about the future and the unknown. Also, progress rarely goes in a straight line. There are often ups and downs, which can be confusing and feel uncomfortable. You may find that you are not where you hoped you would be when finishing this treatment. Therefore, it is essential to look at your progress objectively. In other words, it helps to see your progress as data to inform your decisions rather than as an indicator of who you are. Even if you did not make the gains you had hoped for, you accomplished something great with the effort and energy you put into this treatment, and it may just take more time and practice to get to where you are hoping.

Exercise 8.1: My Progress Assessment

By answering the questions in Exercise 8.1: My Progress Assessment, you will have a better idea of whether you can move on to treatment completion or return to one of the skills. You may photocopy this exercise from the book or download multiple copies at the Treatments *That Work*™ website (www.oxfordclinicalpsych.com/PAT).

If you answered "yes" to items 1 and 2 on Exercise 8.1, then you have successfully completed this treatment. Because of your hard work, you have improved your mood, including increasing the frequency, variety, and intensity of the positive emotions you experience. You are ready to move on to the next section!

If you answered "no" to either items 1 or 2 on Exercise 8.1, then review your answers to questions 4 through 12. If you answered "no" to any skill or chapter, it can be helpful to return to that material for an additional week or two to see if further gains can be made. If you have not noticed additional improvements after a couple of weeks, it may be best to talk to your health care provider about other treatment options.

Overall Treatment Evaluation: Positive Mood

1. Has your overall mood improved since the start of treatment?

2. Are you feeling positive emotions more *frequently*? Are you noticing *more* positive emotions throughout your day or week? Do you feel certain positive emotions *more intensely*?

Overall Treatment Evaluation: Negative Mood

3. What about your negative mood?

Treatment Evaluation: Core Components

Chapter 5: Actions Toward Feeling Better

4. Are you engaging in more meaningful activities? Are you able to savor the activities that you already engage in?

5. Have you been incorporating more positive activities throughout your day and week?

Chapter 6: Attending to the Positive

6. Are you noticing silver linings every day?

7. Are you giving yourself credit for things you did well? Are you accepting praise without dismissing it? Are you attributing some positive events to your own doing?

8. Are you taking time to imagine future events positively?

Chapter 7: Building Positivity

9. Are you having more loving and kind feelings toward yourself and others?

10. Are you noticing feeling joy from the successes and joy of others?

11. Are you feeling more grateful each day, even during times of stress?

12. Are you more generous to others or yourself? Have you been engaging in even tiny acts of generosity (e.g., kindness, helping hand, a listening ear, advice) a few times a week?

Exercise 8.1

My Progress Assessment

Practice Plan

Long-Term Goals

You have improved your mood! Now is the time to think about your goals for after treatment. What was this treatment in service of? Why did you want to improve your mood? Answering some of these questions might help determine what steps to take after treatment. For example, if you completed this treatment in service of being a more present parent, write down concrete steps you can take that will help you continue with that goal moving forward. See Exercise 8.2: My Long-Term Goals, on page 119.

Let's see how Joy is doing:

At the conclusion of treatment, Joy noticed that she experiences positive emotions more frequently and intensely than before. While she reported she still has some occasional ups and downs, she now has a new set of tools to help her deal with them, particularly on days when she is feeling down or with little motivation, interest or joy. More specifically, Joy stated that she has made Gratitude a routine practice and can be more aware of the small things that help improve her mood each day. She also reported that she notices feeling more connected with her husband and children and can engage in more positive activities throughout her week. She started running again, which helps her feel more energetic. When she makes mistakes at work, she focuses on the silver linings. Imagining the Positive has been particularly helpful for her to meet deadlines. She makes sure to savor the moment and to take ownership.

Joy's My Long-Term Goals sheet is shown in Figure 8.1.

My Long-Term Goals

Instructions: Identify at least 1-3 goals that you have for after treatment. What was this treatment in service of? Why did you want to improve your mood? Identify any steps that you need to take to meet each goal. Identify one of the skills from this treatment as a step towards meeting one of your goals.

My long-term goals are...

1. Take ownership for being a good parent

   Step 1. Do 1-2 weekly fun activities with my kids

   Step 2. Make a gratitude list about my kids nightly

   Step 3. Find the silver lining after a tough day

2. Improve relationship with my husband

   Step 1. Have 1 date night per month

   Step 2. Practice loving-kindness toward my husband

   Step 3. Make a gratitude list about my husband nightly

3. Become re-engaged with work

   Step 1. Take ownership of success at work

   Step 2. Build mastery by completing challenging tasks

   Step 3. Find the silver lining after difficult work days

Figure 8.1

Joy's completed My Long-Term Goals sheet.

Exercise 8.2: My Long-Term Goals

Your turn! Using Exercise 8.2, complete your own list of long-term goals. See if each of your steps can hit on at least one of the skills you learned, like in Joy's example.

My Long-Term Goals

Instructions: Identify at least 1-3 goals that you have for after treatment. What was this treatment in service of? Why did you want to improve your mood? Identify any steps that you need to take to meet each goal. Identify one of the skills from this treatment as a step towards meeting one of your goals.

My long-term goals are...

1. _____

    Step 1. _____

    Step 2. _____

    Step 3. _____

2. _____

    Step 1. _____

    Step 2. _____

    Step 3. _____

3. _____

    Step 1. _____

    Step 2. _____

    Step 3. _____

Exercise 8.2

My Long-Term Goals

Progress Maintenance

Maintaining your gains after treatment is over requires continued practice. Just like maintaining muscle mass or weight loss requires continued exercise and healthy eating, practicing your skills on a regular basis will lead to enhanced mood in the long term. Coming up with a plan for how you will maintain your gains will set you up to be successful in the long run. When creating this plan, it can be helpful to break down the steps you will take to maintain the gains you made from each treatment module.

Let's see how Felix is doing:

 Felix found a new job. He is proud of that achievement and is Taking Ownership of his initiative and effort. While he still experiences some low days, he now has a new toolbox of exercises and skills to practice to help him improve his mood. He really liked the Loving-Kindness and Finding the Silver Linings activities during treatment and is using those skills on most days of the week. He noticed that Finding the Silver Linings allows him to take an otherwise gloomy day and notice the positive aspects throughout. He also enjoys regularly scheduling positive activities such as going on walks, having coffee with a friend, or just listening to one of his favorite songs. Felix has learned to feel grateful for those moments and to savor them. He also has practiced activities that build mastery, such as teaching himself to write music with new software, or completing simpler tasks like going to the grocery store and cleaning. He now regularly reaches out to friends and offers help to neighbors.

What steps will he take to maintain his progress? Figure 8.2 shows Felix's completed Maintaining My Gains sheet.

Maintaining My Gains

Instructions: Answer each of these questions. Identify how you will maintain your gains in treatment through skills from Actions Toward Feeling Better, Attending to the Positive, and Building Positivity.

How will I maintain my gains through *Actions Toward Feeling Better?*
1. I will call my friend twice per week
2. I will spend at least 1 hour applying for jobs each week
3. I will spend at least 20 min of each day outside

How will I maintain my gains through *Attending to the Positive?*
1. I will find the silver lining after a difficult day
2. I will take ownership when I do things well
3. I will imagine the positive before engaging with friends

How will I maintain my gains through *Building Positivity?*
1. I will make a gratitude list about my family members
2. I will volunteer in my community
3. I will practice loving-kindness toward myself

Figure 8.2

Felix's completed Maintaining My Gains exercise.

Exercise 8.3: Maintaining My Gains

Using Exercise 8.3: Maintaining My Gains, identify what you will do to maintain the gains you've already made. You may photocopy this exercise from the book or download multiple copies at the Treatments *That Work*™ website (www.oxfordclinicalpsych.com/PAT).

Maintaining My Gains

Instructions: Answer each of these questions. Identify how you will maintain your gains in treatment through skills from Actions Toward Feeling Better, Attending to the Positive, and Building Positivity.

How will I maintain my gains through *Actions Toward Feeling Better?*

1. _____

2. _____

3. _____

How will I maintain my gains through *Attending to the Positive?*

1. _____

2. _____

3. _____

How will I maintain my gains through *Building Positivity?*

1. _____

2. _____

3. _____

Exercise 8.3

Maintaining My Gains

Research has shown that continued practice after treatment is over reduces the risk of relapse. Imagine what would happen if you had stopped driving just after getting your driver's license. You would most likely lose some of your ability to drive. Behavioral and thinking skills are similar: They require continued practice so that they become second nature, just like driving. Expect that there will be challenging situations. Imagine that a child unexpectedly crosses the road in front of your car. If you drive daily, it will be easier to react than if you are out of practice. Likewise, it is easier to handle life challenges and natural mood fluctuations if you continue to use your skills after treatment is over.

Moving forward:

- What do you anticipate getting in the way of practicing these skills?
- What do you expect to trip you up?
- Which are the more difficult skills for you?
- What stressful experiences make it more difficult for you to practice certain skills?

Exercise 8.4: Overcoming Barriers will help you address these questions. Figure 8.3 is an example completed by Joy.

Overcoming Barriers

Instructions: Identify possible barriers that might interfere with you meeting one of your long-term goals. List 1-3 steps you can take to avoid that barrier.

Barriers...

1. _Getting busy with work_

    Step 1. _Find time 1x/wk to review my skills_

    Step 2. _Schedule 2+ positive activities into my week_

    Step 3. _Spend 5 mins in morning identifying my silver linings_

2. _Notice a decrease in mood following a stressful week_

    Step 1. _Schedule 1 positive activity per day_

    Step 2. _Complete a gratitude list about my family_

    Step 3. _Take ownership of successes at work_

3. _Become stressed due to family requirements_

    Step 1. _Schedule 2+ positive activities into my week_

    Step 2. _Spend 5 mins practicing loving-kindness each week_

    Step 3. _Imagine the positive before a family event_

Figure 8.3

Joy's completed Overcoming Barriers exercise.

Now it's your turn! Using Exercise 8.4: Overcoming Barriers, identify as many potential barriers as you can. If you need more room, you may photocopy this exercise from the book or download multiple copies at the Treatments *That Work*™ website (www.oxfordclinicalpsych.com/PAT). Then, for each barrier, list one to three steps you can take to avoid it. This might include things like scheduling regular time in your day to practice, setting reminders on your phone, reviewing your workbook once a week or month, and continuing to practice the more difficult skills by writing them down in your workbook.

Overcoming Barriers

Instructions: Identify possible barriers that might interfere with you meeting one of your long-term goals. List 1-3 steps you can take to avoid that barrier.

Barriers...

1. _____

    Step 1. _____

    Step 2. _____

    Step 3. _____

2. _____

    Step 1. _____

    Step 2. _____

    Step 3. _____

3. _____

    Step 1. _____

    Step 2. _____

    Step 3. _____

Exercise 8.4

Overcoming Barriers

Changing behavior and forming new habits is difficult, especially when the old habits have become so automatic after years of doing them. Therefore, expect that there will be moments when you fall back into old habits, especially during times of stress. These slips are called lapses. They are expected to happen and are okay. They are not a sign of failure or cause for concern. When you notice these lapses, we encourage you to be compassionate with yourself, recognize them as lapses, and then take steps forward by continuing to practice your skills. Continuing to practice skills is essential to maintaining gains.

Lapses are different from relapses. While lapses are brief, relapses span days or weeks. A relapse is a return to pretreatment levels of positive or negative mood. Using the exercises in this chapter will help to avoid relapses.

Review My Long-Term Goals (Exercise 8.2), Maintaining My Gains (Exercise 8.3), and Overcoming Barriers (Exercise 8.4) regularly, and if you believe you might be experiencing a relapse instead of a lapse, talk to your health care provider.

If you feel some anxiety about ending treatment, this is quite usual. Refer back to the exercises in this workbook regularly. Feel free to make copies of the exercises from the Treatments *That Work*™ website (www.oxfordclinicalpsych.com/PAT), and put them in a place that is regularly accessible to review as needed. Remember, you—and only you—have made success in this treatment possible because of the work you have done. This means that you are capable of maintaining your gains after treatment. In this final session, it may be helpful to practice two skills—*Taking Ownership* and *Imagining the Positive*—to highlight the gains you've made and to help you envision a positive future.

When to Seek Additional Help

PAT has been shown to enhance positive emotions and reduce negative emotions in individuals who experience anhedonia and clinical levels of depression, stress, and anxiety. It also decreases suicidal behaviors. It is natural to hope that you will never experience those symptoms again. You may even ask yourself, "Am I now healed?" Those are difficult questions to answer. Research has shown that emotional disorders can recur. Depression, for example, is an episodic disorder. This means individuals who suffer from it can improve significantly and be well for a long time. Some however will experience another episode at some point in their lives. As we mentioned earlier, now that you have learned and applied the skills taught in this treatment, you can graduate to continue using them independently. Like any newly learned skill, it is essential to be mindful that the work is not finished and has just begun. Imagine that you learned a new language and never practiced it after you receive your certificate, or never drove again after you receive your driver's license. You would forget your skills and would not be ready if you need them.

Similarly, after completing treatment, expect that hard times will come. You will be better prepared to handle them if you have continued practicing the skills that have helped you improve positive emotions and reduce negative ones the most.

However, sometimes it will not be enough to use your skills. In this situation, you may require additional help. If you worked with a therapist, it could be helpful to schedule a booster session. One or two sessions may be sufficient for you to get back on track. If you worked on your own, you might want to seek help using an evidence-based psychotherapist. We provide a list of resources at the end of this chapter. Alternatively, you may try medications under the supervision of a health care provider or a combination of medication and psychotherapy.

Don't wait until your systems have become overwhelmed. Watch out for triggers and signs that you are getting worse. One way is to keep a diary with a mood rating. Keep in mind that emotional disorders are very treatable disorders, and just like any disorder, the earlier you treat it, the quicker the recovery.

Final Words of Encouragement

Congratulations! You have now completed the Positive Affect Treatment (PAT). Not only have you mastered each skill, but you also identified and problem-solved potential pitfalls. You have become your own therapist. This is a sign of true success.

We are grateful that you allowed us to provide you with skills that we genuinely hope were helpful for you. You are now equipped with a toolbox full of skills and techniques. You have worked hard over the course of treatment to improve your positive mood. Take ownership and savor the moment! Reward yourself with a positive activity or gift, and be mindful of the road ahead of you. There will be gloomy days, but remember the silver linings and your ability to master and improve your situation through the continued practice of changing your thoughts, behaviors, and feelings. We wish you all the best for your journey ahead!

List of Resources for Individuals with Depression and Anxiety

American Psychological Association: APA is a professional and scientific organization that represents psychologists in the United States. It provides information for psychologists who are researchers, educators, clinicians, consultants, and students. Additionally, APA has a Psychology Help Center, which is a resource for the public that provides information and articles related to daily physical and emotional well-being. https://www.apa.org/helpcenter

Anxiety and Depression Association of America: ADAA is a nonprofit organization that is dedicated to the prevention and treatment of anxiety, depression, obsessive–compulsive disorder, and related disorders. ADAA provides resources for individuals interested in learning more about evidence-based interventions for anxiety disorders and depression and provides resources to assist in finding a therapist. https://adaa.org/

Association for Behavioral and Cognitive Therapies: ABCT is an organization that is dedicated to the improvement of mental health by utilizing evidence-based cognitive, behavioral, and biological principles. https://www.abct.org/Home/ ABCT also provides resources for individuals in the community looking to find a therapist specializing in cognitive–behavioral therapy based on ZIP code, state, specialty, and insurance information. https://www.findcbt.org/FAT/

Alicia E. Meuret, PhD, is a Professor at the Department of Psychology at Southern Methodist University (SMU), the Director of the SMU Anxiety and Depression Research Center, and a licensed clinical psychologist. She completed her doctoral studies at Stanford University Department of Psychiatry and Behavioral Sciences and her postdoctoral studies at the Affective Neuroscience Laboratory at Harvard University and the Center for Anxiety and Related Disorders at Boston University. Her research program focuses on novel treatment approaches for anxiety and mood disorders, biomarkers in anxiety disorders and chronic disease (asthma), fear extinction mechanisms of exposure therapy, and mediators and moderators in individuals with affective dysregulations, including non-suicidal self-injury. Dr. Meuret is the founder of Capnometry-Assisted Respiratory Training (CART). Dr. Meuret has published over 100 scientific publications and authored over 200 conference presentations. Her work has received ongoing funding from the National Institutes of Health and other funding agencies. She has received multiple honors, including from the Anxiety and Depression Association of America, the Psychiatric Research Society, and the American Psychosomatic Society. She is a Beck Institute Fellow and a Rotunda Outstanding Professor. Dr. Meuret is a member of the Scientific Advisory Board of the Anxiety and Depression Association of America, was past president of the International Society of the Advancement of Respiratory Psychophysiology, and is a fellow of the Association of Cognitive and Behavioral Therapies. As a technical expert, she assisted the Agency for Healthcare Research and Quality Effective Health Care Program and was on the Scientific Advisory Board of the Centre for Excellence at the University of Leuven, Belgium. Dr. Meuret serves on several editorial boards and was an Associate Editor for Behavior Therapy. Dr. Meuret has more than 20 years of clinical experience treating patients with emotional disorders.

Halina J. Dour, PhD, is the owner of the Center for Genuine Growth, a multi-state telepsychology practice. Dr. Dour spent most of her postdoctoral career within Veterans Affairs (VA) healthcare systems. She served as the Eating Disorder Team Coordinator and as a member of the PTSD

Clinical Team within the Orlando VA Healthcare System. Prior to this, she spent nearly two years as a clinical psychologist in the Mental Health Clinic and Intensive Outpatient Program at the VA Puget Sound, Seattle Division. Dr. Dour has been trained in numerous evidence-based treatments and worked in a variety of settings. This, coupled with a passion for creating interventions, therapy materials, and programming, has led Dr. Dour to gain a specific expertise in treatment and program development. She has served, and continues to serve, as a consultant on multiple treatment development projects. Dr. Dour received her bachelor's degree *cum laude* in psychology from Wellesley College and her PhD in Clinical Psychology from the University of California, Los Angeles, where she studied under the mentorship of Dr. Michelle Craske. During her doctoral training, she earned numerous awards and fellowships, including the National Science Foundation Fellowship, the University Distinguished Fellowship, the Ursula-Mandel Stipend Award, the Philip & Aida Siff Award, the UCLA Affiliates Award, the Senior Clinical Scientist Award, the Outstanding SSCP Student Clinician Award, and the APA Div12 Distinguished Student Practice in Clinical Psychology Award. Dr. Dour completed her predoctoral internship at the VA Sepulveda Ambulatory Care Center and her postdoctoral fellowship at the VA Puget Sound, Seattle Division.

Amanda G. Loerinc Guinyard, PhD, is the Founder and Executive Director of the CBT Center of Boston and is a licensed clinical psychologist in Massachusetts, California, and Connecticut. In her practice, she provides CBT and adherent DBT to adults and adolescents in the greater Boston area and via telehealth to individuals in California and Connecticut. Additionally, she provides consultation and training in both CBT and DBT to psychologists and other mental health professionals across the country, and is a Diplomate of the Academy of Cognitive and Behavioral Therapies. Most recently, Dr. Loerinc Guinyard served as the Assistant Clinical Director at CBT California, where she oversaw clinical staff, supervised trainees, and provided consultation and training to staff at the practice and professionals in the Los Angeles community. Dr. Loerinc Guinyard graduated *cum laude* from Boston University with a major in psychology and received her PhD from the University of California, Los Angeles (UCLA) under the mentorship of Dr. Michelle Craske. She completed her APA-accredited predoctoral internship at the VA Sepulveda Ambulatory Care Center in North Hills, California, and her postdoctoral fellowship at CBT California.

Michelle G. Craske, PhD, is Professor of Psychology, Psychiatry and Biobehavioral Sciences, Miller Endowed Term Chair, Director of the Anxiety and Depression Research Center, and Associate Director of the Staglin Family Music Center for Behavioral and Brain Health, at the University of California, Los Angeles. She is also co-director of the UCLA Depression Grand Challenge. She has researched and published extensively in the area of fear, anxiety, and depression and is on the Web of Science Most Highly Cited Researcher List. She has been the recipient of extramural funding for research projects pertaining to risk factors for anxiety and depression among children and adolescents, neural mediators of emotion regulation and behavioral treatments for anxiety disorders, fear extinction translational models for optimizing exposure therapy, novel behavioral therapies targeting reward sensitivity and anhedonia, and scalable treatment models for underserved populations. She has received multiple awards of distinction. At UCLA, she received the Society of Postdoctoral Scholars at UCLA Mentorship Award and Career Development Award. Nationally, she received the American Psychological Association Society for a Science of Clinical Psychology Distinguished Scientist Award, the Outstanding Researcher Award from the Association for Behavioral and Cognitive Therapy, and the Aaron T. Beck Award from the Academy of Cognitive Therapy. Internationally, she was awarded the International Francqui Professorship from Belgium, and the Eleonore Trefftz Guest Professorship Award from the Technical University of Dresden, Germany. She received an honorary doctorate from Maastricht University, Netherlands, and is an honorary fellow of the Department of Psychiatry, Oxford University, and an honorary fellow of the Dutch-Flemish Postgraduate School for Research and Education. Further, she has been president of the APA Society for a Science of Clinical Psychology and the Association for Behavioral and Cognitive Therapy. She is Editor-in-Chief for *Behaviour Research and Therapy*. Dr. Craske received her BA Hons from the University of Tasmania and her PhD from the University of British Columbia.